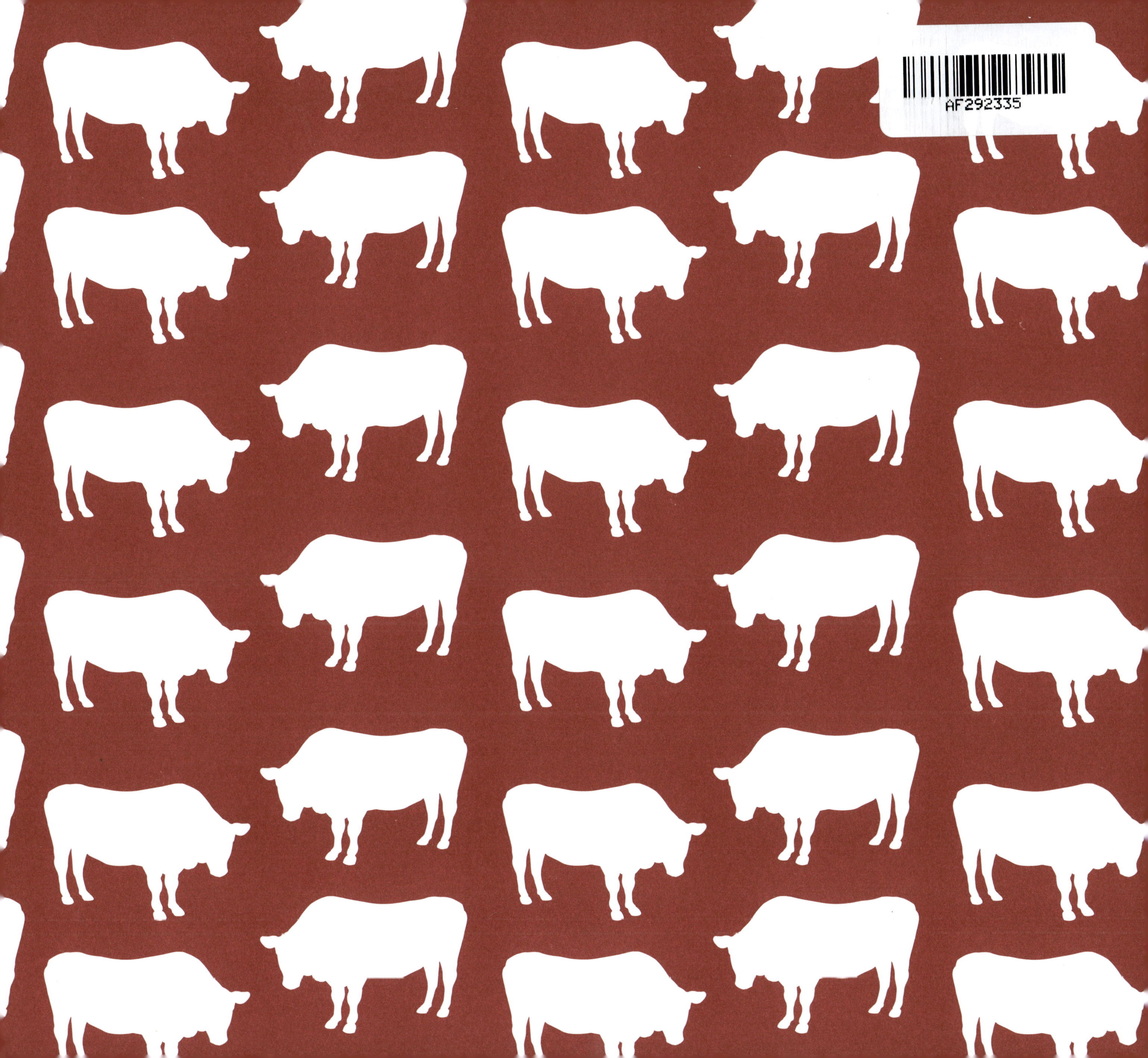
AF292335

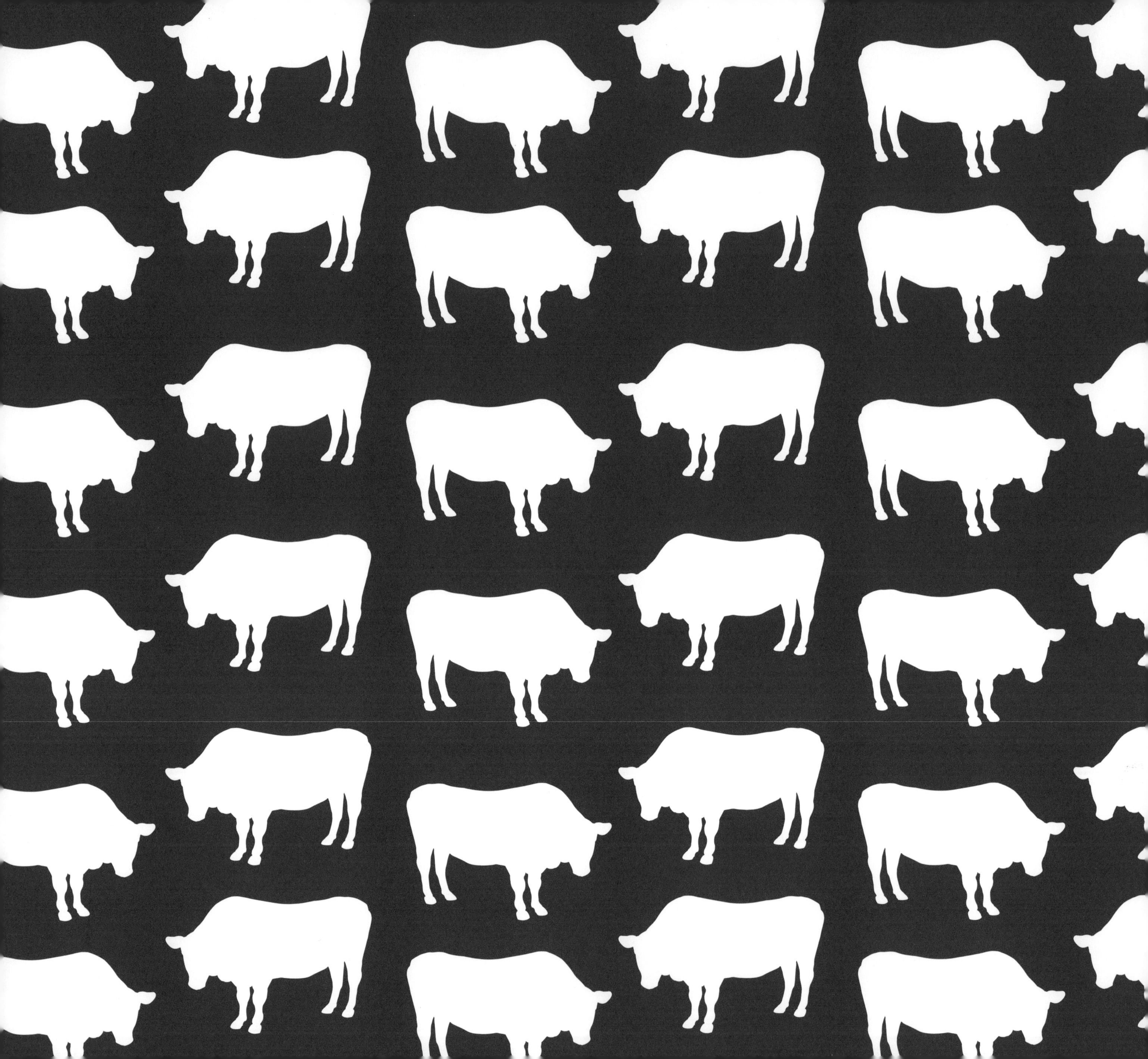

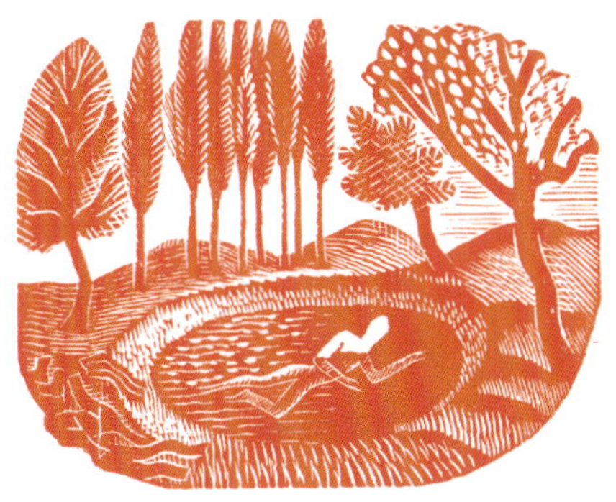

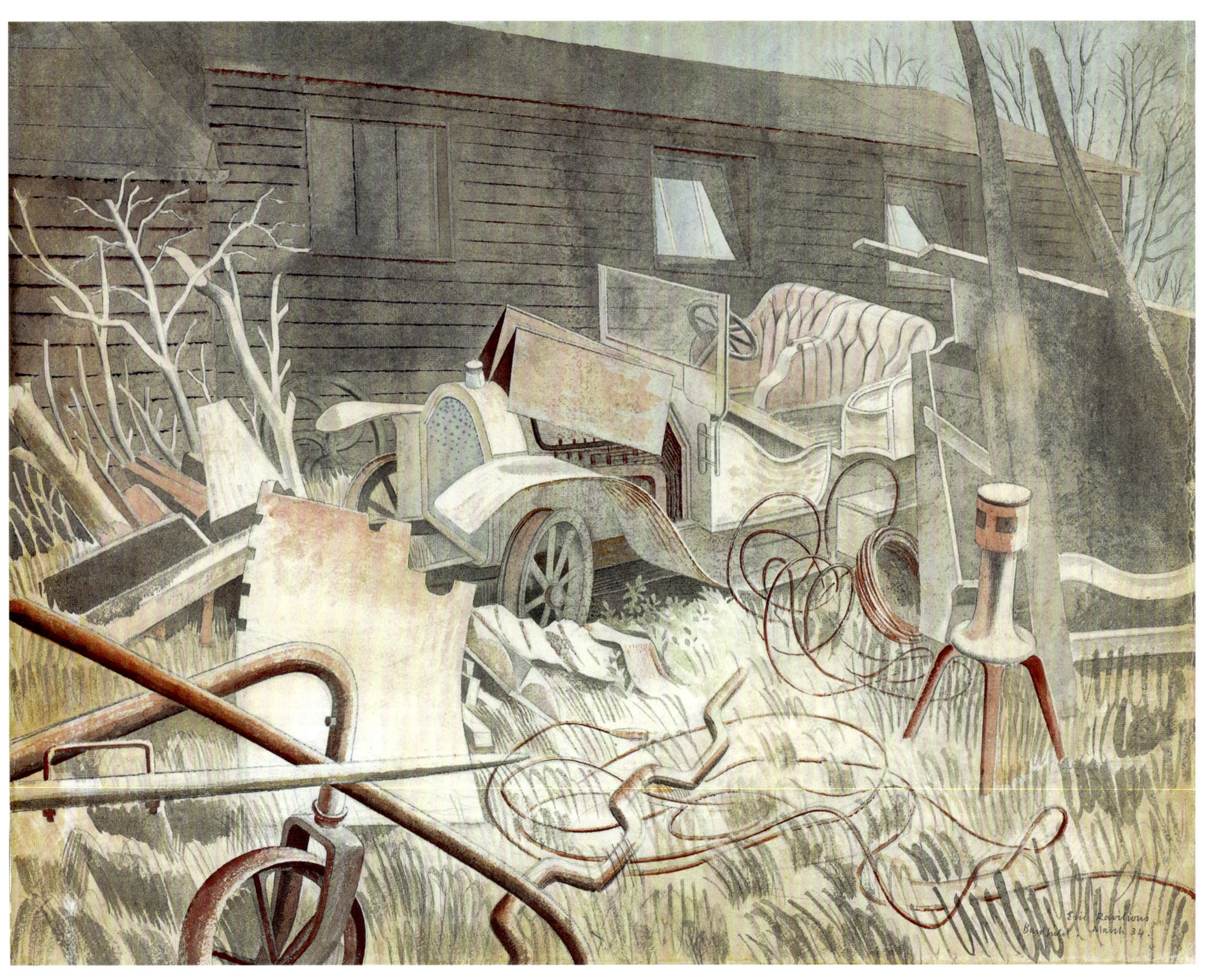

Talbot-Darracq, 1934, watercolour, 45.7 x 55.9 cm, Towner Art Gallery, Eastbourne.

James Russell

RAVILIOUS IN PICTURES
A COUNTRY LIFE

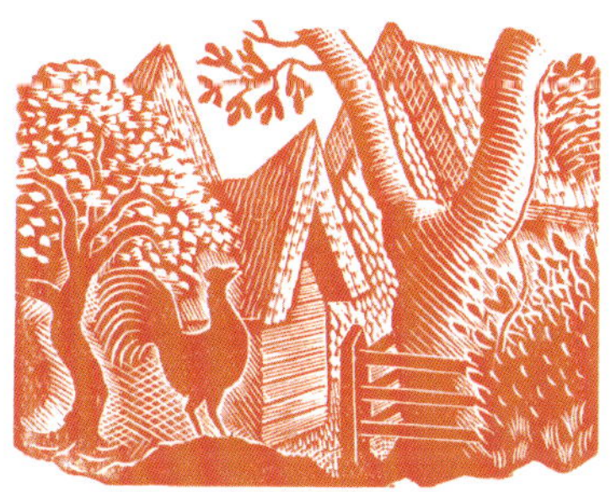

The Mainstone Press

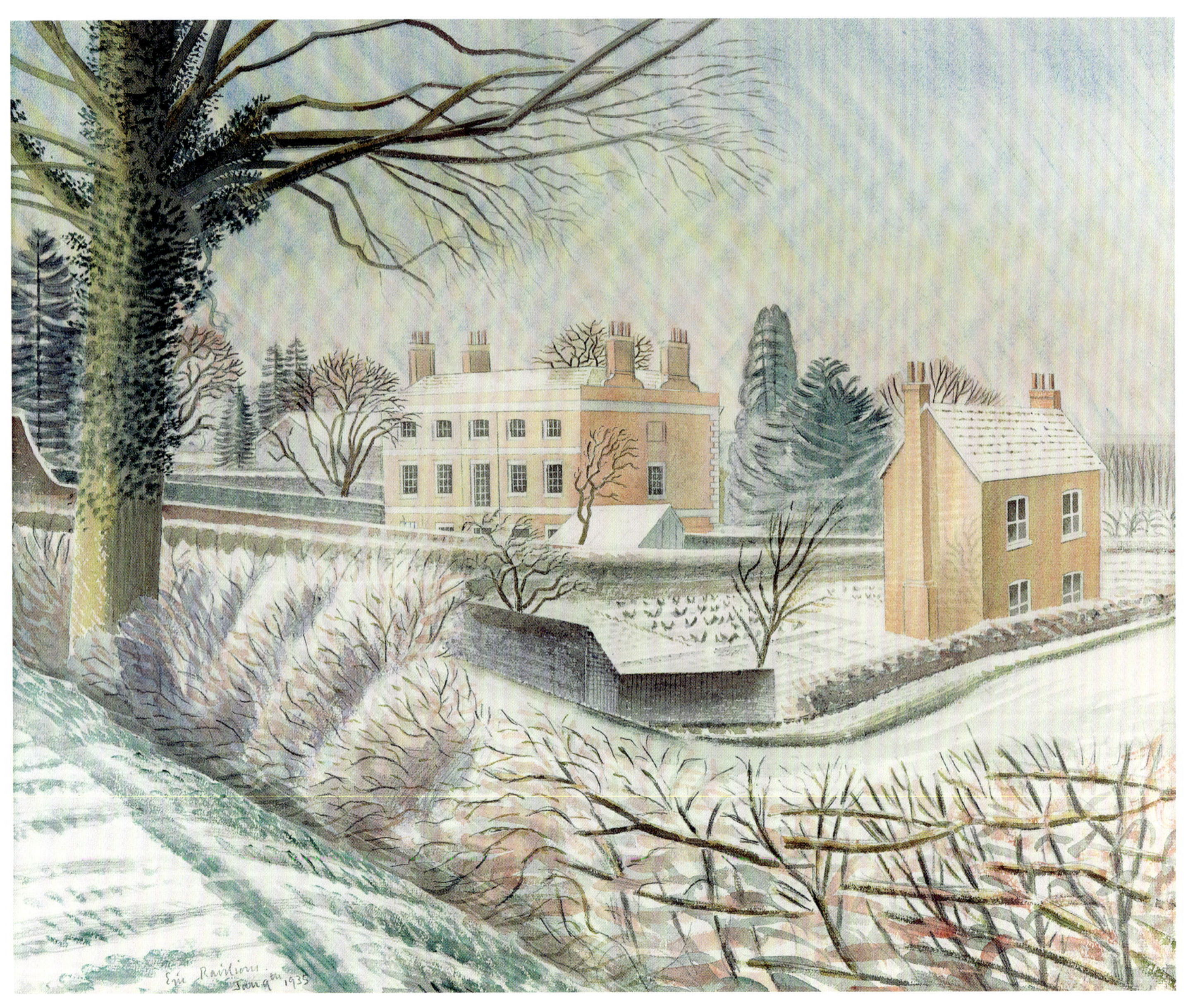

Vicarage in Winter, 1935, watercolour, 46 x 56.5 cm, private collection.

INTRODUCTION

In 1932 Eric Ravilious moved with his wife Tirzah from London to Great Bardfield in Essex, and for the remaining decade of his life they lived within an easy cycle ride of the village, first in Castle Hedingham and then at Ironbridge Farm, near Shalford. It was in north-west Essex that his children were born, and it was here that he found the inspiration for a series of watercolours that together form a remarkable portrait of country life in the 1930s.

This volume, the third in the *Ravilious in Pictures* series, features twenty-two watercolours, accompanied by essays that explore the content and context of the paintings, from the history of particular buildings and industries to more personal stories about family and friends. Drawing on letters, diaries and interviews, *Ravilious in Pictures: A Country Life* offers an intimate, funny and moving portrait of the artist at home.

Ravilious was introduced to Essex by Edward Bawden, who was raised in Braintree. When the two men met in 1922, at the Design School of the Royal College of Art (RCA) in London, they immediately became firm friends, and over the following years they travelled regularly to north-west Essex, exploring the countryside and looking for subjects to paint. A weekend retreat became, as we shall see, a permanent home and the birthplace of the Great Bardfield art colony. But before this, in 1930, they achieved a remarkable coup, when Prime Minister Stanley Baldwin unveiled the murals they had painted together at Morley College in London. This success brought them national recognition and introduced them to patrons like Geoffrey Fry – the Prime Minister's Private Secretary – and his wife Alathea. With a potential audience established, they began to explore landscape painting in earnest.

Some years earlier, as a young man studying at the Eastbourne School of Art, Ravilious had encountered the radiant, meticulously designed paintings of 18th-century landscape watercolourist Francis Towne. Far from being part of the artistic establishment, Towne was one of several figures – others included John Sell Cotman and Samuel Palmer – who were rediscovered in the early 20th century. This was particularly true of Palmer, whose extraordinary pastoral visions of 1825–35 had rarely been shown publicly until the Victoria and Albert Museum staged a major retrospective in 1926. Ravilious and Bawden were so taken with this thrilling new body of work that they made a pilgrimage to Palmer's home in Shoreham, Kent.

Inspired by these artists of the past whose vision seemed so modern, Ravilious and Bawden became fascinated by landscape painting and by watercolour, a medium Paul Nash championed when, as a part-time tutor, he taught Ravilious and Bawden at the RCA. Nash wrestled throughout his career with the problem of reconciling 'going modern' with 'being British', and he was not alone in seeking forms of expression that were both contemporary and rooted in a particular place. Spurred on by the example of Towne and others, Ravilious used watercolour to portray distinctive subjects in his own style, sketching an abandoned bus or a train going over a bridge with a peculiar clarity of vision. Mesmerised, critics described how Ravilious made them feel that they were seeing familiar things for the first time.

For the artist, finding suitable subjects was a constant occupation, and what attracted him to Essex was perhaps less the landscape than the continuing survival in that isolated region of human enterprise on an intimate scale. While towns and cities were rapidly modernising, with chain stores taking over the high street and cars taking over the roads, the villages of rural Essex remained essentially local, pedestrian, and old-fashioned.

Raised in his father's Eastbourne antique shop, Ravilious found inspiration not only in distinctive buildings and scenes, but also in oddities and relics of the past, many of which he found around Great Bardfield and the Hedinghams. The livestock and antiquated machinery of local farms provided a rich source of subject matter, as did the 'sweet uneventful countryside' described by John Betjeman in his poem, *Essex*:

> *Like streams the little by-roads run*
> *Through oats and barley round a hill*
> *To where blue willows catch the sun*
> *By some white weather-boarded mill.*

Betjeman wrote this after World War II, inspired by images in an Edwardian picture book. This Essex was lost to the poet, but not to Ravilious working only a few years earlier; grain was still being ground at the mill he found, and bricks were still made at the brickworks.

But though country life was slow-moving and conservative, it was also fashionable. The work of country writers like Edward Thomas, W. H. Hudson and H. J. Massingham was popular and influential, while new editions of the celebrated 18th-century naturalist Gilbert White of Selborne appeared at regular intervals through the 1930s — Ravilious himself illustrated one. And people did not just read about village life, they set out to experience it. As Alexandra Harris puts it in her 2010 book *Romantic Moderns*: 'If a Domesday Book had been compiled in the late 1930s, recording the inhabitants of villages and outlying farms, it would include most of the major figures of English art and letters.'

From Virginia Woolf and Evelyn Waugh to John Piper, Stanley Spencer and Ravilious himself, writers and artists swapped urban pollution, unrest and disease for the pleasures and trials of rural life. The railway system allowed people to come and go, as Ravilious did, teaching a few days in London then perhaps travelling on to the Sussex Downs to make new sketches before returning to Essex. Yet he and Tirzah were not aloof from life in the village. Rather, their letters and diaries show how closely they were involved with the people around them. In the paintings too, we see real people whose lives have otherwise gone unrecorded, but who are shown here engaged in their everyday lives, whether preparing a joint of meat, waiting for the baker's cart, or riding a bicycle across a village square.

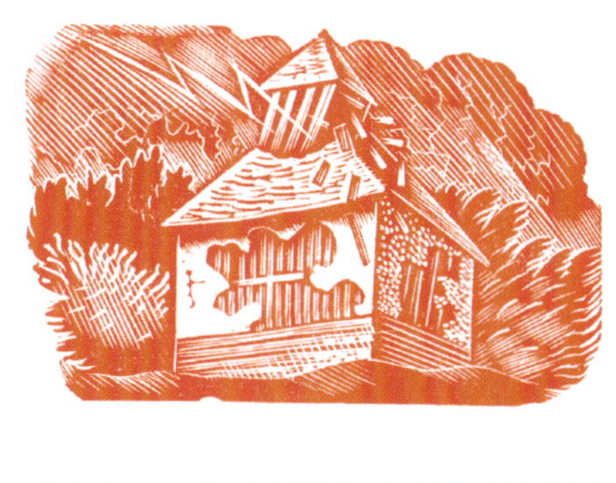

THE PAINTINGS

PROSPECT FROM AN ATTIC

A bright morning sun illuminates rooftiles and trees, greenhouses and warm red brick. It lights the open door of a shed and the sheaves of straw propped up against the wall, and a woman brandishing a walking stick over a rug. Vibrant and optimistic, this is a fine prospect, although it is not from an attic but from the roof above. But what was Eric Ravilious doing on this village rooftop in 1932?

Ten years earlier he had enrolled in the Design School of the Royal College of Art, London, where his fellow students included the hard-working, introspective Edward Bawden. Though very different characters, the two men, both shopkeeper's sons, shared artistic tastes and a waspish sense of humour. As artists they were often referred to in the same breath, as they both excelled in mural painting and watercolour.

'Eric admired Edward's dour creativeness, his sheer professionalism,' their RCA friend Douglas Percy Bliss explained, 'and Edward believed in the elegance and fastidious taste with which Eric was endowed. They worked together in perfect amity.'

After graduation the friends began exploring the countryside around Bawden's home town of Braintree, Essex, looking for subjects to paint, and in 1930 they decided to find a more permanent base. One summer morning they took a train to the village of Great Dunmow, then hired bicycles and set off into the countryside. At Thaxted they tried unsuccessfully to rent the deserted-looking town hall. They had no better luck elsewhere, until finally they cycled up the little rise to the centre of Great Bardfield and saw, next to the police station, a Georgian house of red and black brick, with a mansard roof and a white front door.

The panes of the windows had been daubed with circles of whitewash and, taking this as a sign, the two friends enquired at a nearby teashop and discovered that a retired stewardess from an ocean liner lived there. Mrs Kinnear was her name, and she agreed to rent them two rooms on the ground floor and two above, with a share of the kitchen and the primitive amenities.

'There was no water,' Edward Bawden recollected later, 'no electricity, no drains. Very exciting. If you're young! We pumped our water from a contaminated well, we had a lavatory outside with three holes showing how important the house was, and oil lamps indoors.'

When Bawden married in 1932 his father bought the whole of Brick House as a wedding present. The roof needed immediate attention, and when the ladders went up both Bawden and Ravilious took the opportunity to draw from this vantage point.

As Tirzah Ravilious remembered it, 'They painted several pictures very early in the morning from the roof of their house, and on one occasion had to come down, nearly overpowered by the smell of kippers cooking for breakfast.'

Prospect from an Attic, 1932, watercolour, 48.3 x 63.5 cm, Scarborough Museums and Gallery.

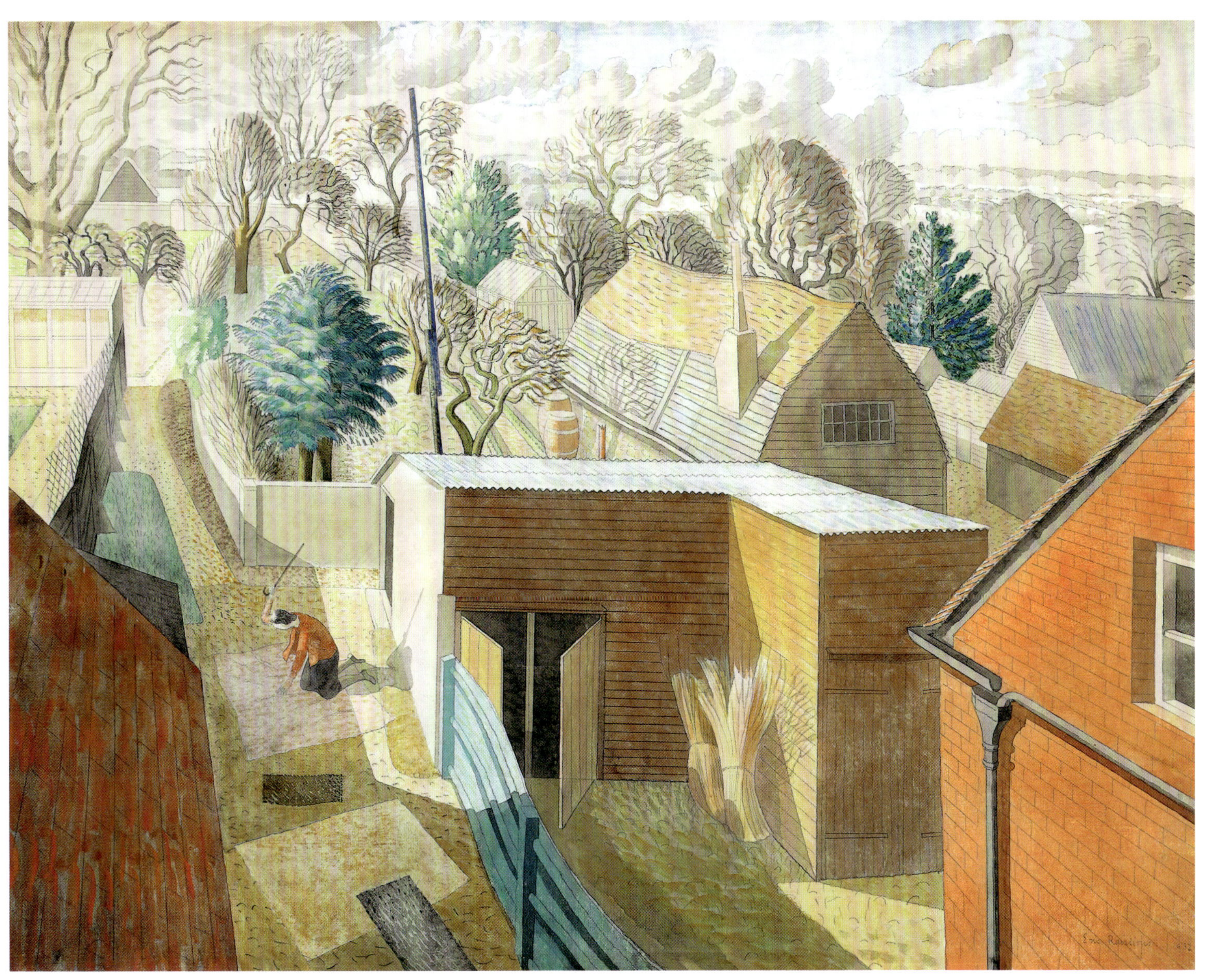

TWO WOMEN IN A GARDEN

Edward Bawden's bride was Charlotte Epton, a former RCA student and a talented potter and painter. As cheerful and outgoing as Bawden was reticent, she proved his ideal match, and, since Brick House was a large house, they invited Ravilious and Tirzah to live with them (while keeping their London flat). Here is Charlotte reading in a deckchair in the shade of the walnut tree, while Tirzah prepares vegetables, perhaps for the kind of outdoor meal Bawden depicted in his illustrations for Ambrose Heath's *Good Food* (1932). An abandoned umbrella adds a wry note.

After years spent living in London they all relished country sights and sounds, from the rare butterflies that drifted into the garden, to swallows building their nests in the portico above the front door and, after heavy rain, the road outside covered with hundreds of little frogs. Inspired by their surroundings, Bawden and Ravilious worked hard, 'competing with one another,' as Tirzah remembered, 'in conditions of various hardships, such as ghastly weather, or having the sun bang in their eyes.'

The women ran the house, taking turns to prepare meals. On her marriage, Charlotte willingly scaled down her artistic ambitions and became renowned as a popular hostess and excellent cook. Tirzah had less enthusiasm for household chores, finding them neither easy nor congenial, but proved a devoted wife and mother. Well established as a wood engraver when she married Ravilious, she abandoned this career, although she did help her husband paint murals at the Midland Hotel, Morecambe in 1933. Only after his death, when her children were older, did she return to fine art in her own right, creating a series of exquisitely coloured, haunting oil paintings.

With all this creative talent on offer, Brick House was decorated in style. 'Edward and Rav are at Bardfield this week,' Charlotte wrote in the spring of 1932, 'decorating the "Victorian" room. They are threatening to paint stags' horns and trophies of the chase in suitable positions on the wall, and forget-me-nots and pansies round the fireplace, but I think Rav will keep a discreet hand over Edward's rococo spirit.'

Bawden had previously created beautiful wallpaper designs for the Curwen Press, and now he went to work on the house. At the same time Charlotte and Tirzah began making marbled papers, using them both for decoration and to cover lampshades and waste-paper baskets, for sale at Muriel Rose's Little Gallery in London. When Peggy Angus, an old friend from RCA days, visited Brick House in 1933, she was dazzled by lozenges of marbled papers, repeated as patchwork patterns in the hall and passage. The dining room, she recalled, was decorated with a wallpaper of brass rubbings, while the parlour gave one the impression of being in a cane structure, surrounded by birdcages and birds.

Two Women in a Garden, 1933, watercolour, 44.4 x 55.5 cm, Fry Art Gallery, Saffron Walden.

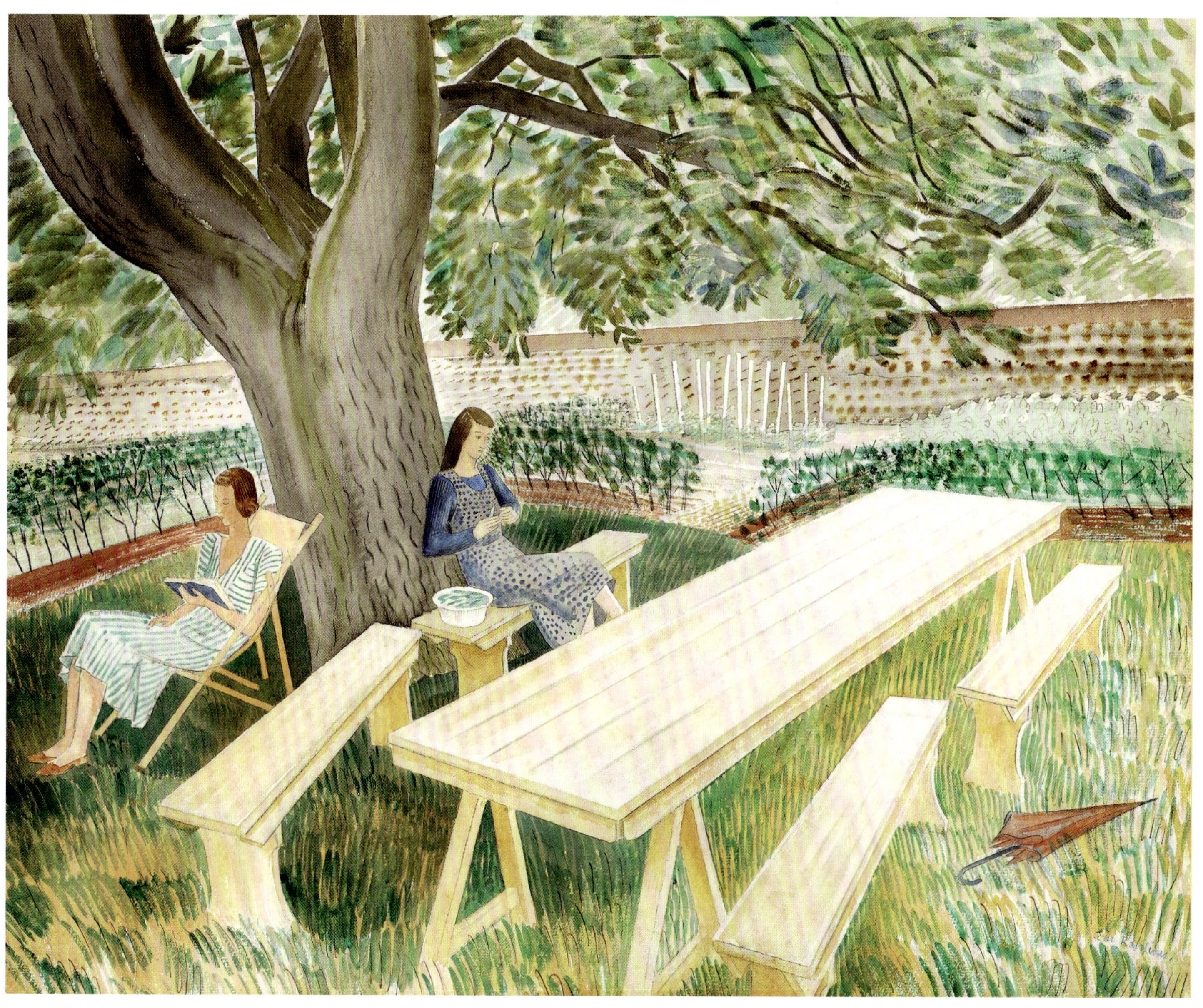

THE ATTIC BEDROOM

ight floods into an attic room, illuminating a fascinating array of objects, from the folding bed with its rippling canvas to a bag of billiard cues. The walls are curiously angled, fitting within the mansard roof of Brick House, so that the poles leaning against the wall to the left stand straight upright yet cast bold, angled shadows. Of the lifebuoy hanging in the window Ravilious has made a strange heavenly body resembling a crescent moon.

The room is full of clues to the life of Brick House. The plants bathed in light from the window testify to Edward Bawden's passion for gardening, which he shared with John Aldridge and other Great Bardfield artists. The lifebuoy, meanwhile, could be a relic of the stewardess's past, although it also reminds us that a path leads across the fields at the back of Brick House to the bank of the River Pant, a meandering Essex stream that becomes, in its lower reaches, the River Blackwater.

When Bawden saw this painting for the first time, at a 1987 exhibition, he recalled that the paddle leaning against the wall belonged to a punt made by one of Tirzah's uncles, from canvas stretched over a wooden frame. This rudimentary craft could be carried easily across the meadows at the end of the garden and set afloat on the gently flowing stream. 'Two of us sat on the bottom,' Bawden remembered, 'facing each other and scooping plenty of water into each other's laps.'

Waterborne explorations were just one feature of the idyllic life enjoyed by the two couples before they had children. Their many visitors were entertained in a wonderfully eccentric manner, as Mary Branson, an old friend from college days, reported. When she visited during the summer, they spent the morning painting a barn down the road before coming home for an energetic game of ping-pong on a table that took up most of the living room.

'After a time Eppie came in with delicious hot-pots,' she wrote, 'and we sat around with soup bowls on the ping-pong table and on our knees. What delicious flavours! One afternoon the Boy [Ravilious] insisted on going to the bottom of the garden where there was a stream. He insisted on bathing with not a stitch on – not so odd when one remembers that we all lived in life classes male and female.'

Ravilious seems not to have worried that the village bobby lived next door to Brick House, but on one occasion Constable Baker did happen upon a similar bathing party. He was, however, too embarrassed to intervene, and today the image of happy swimmers and hesitant policeman is remembered in a delightful linocut by the Bawdens' son Richard, whose birth heralded the beginning of a new chapter in the lives of both couples.

The Attic Bedroom, 1934, watercolour, 44.5 x 62.5 cm, Fry Art Gallery, Saffron Walden.

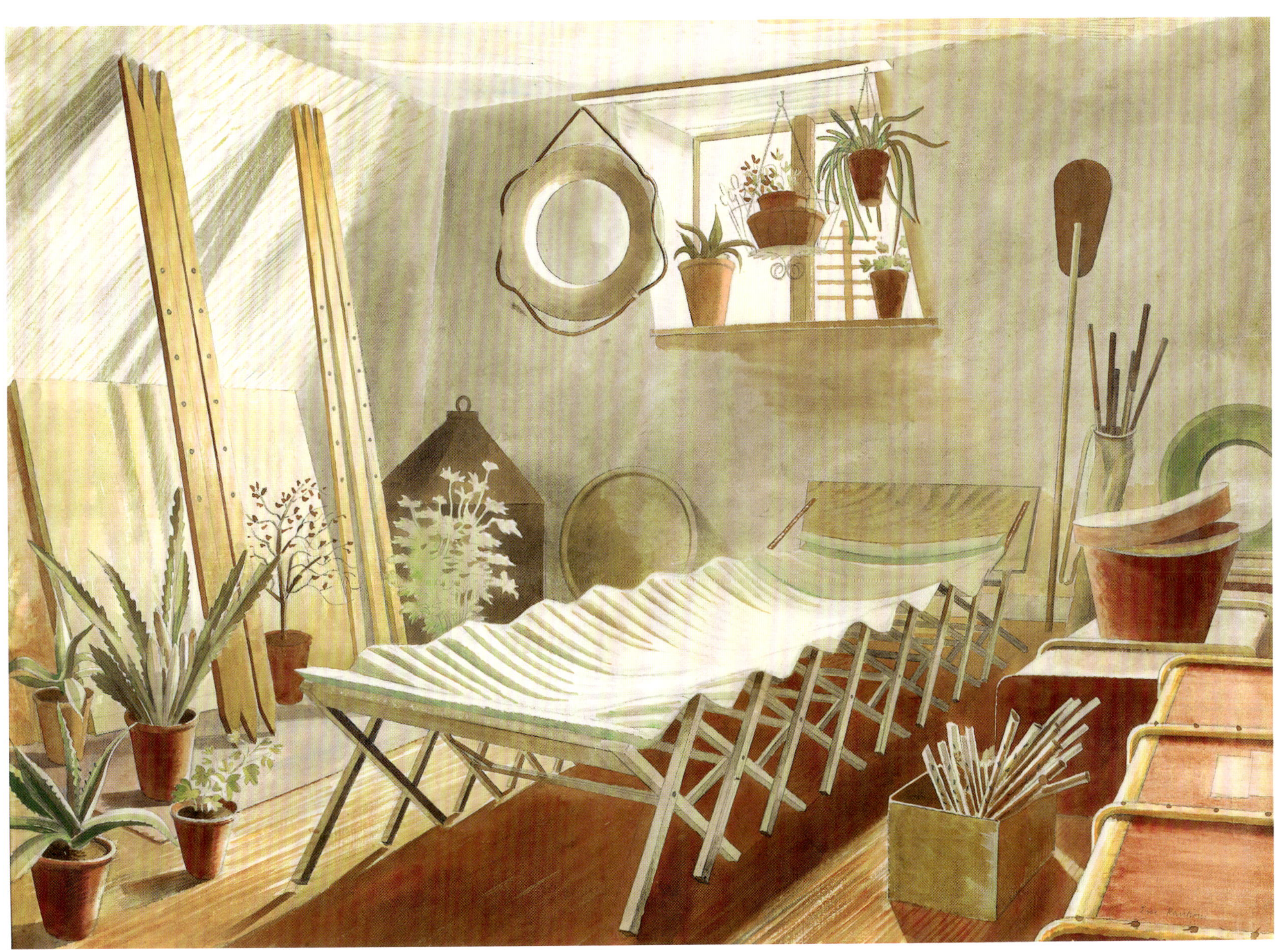

TRACTOR

Ravilious sought unusual subjects outside Brick House as well as within, and found plenty to inspire him. Seven miles from the nearest railway station and with a population of less than a thousand, Great Bardfield was slow to change, so that even in the 1940s a car was a rarity. Farming also evolved only gradually, and this steam powered tractor was probably still in use when Ravilious found it. Steam tractors were being manufactured into the 1930s, and vehicles like this one – built a decade or so earlier by John Fowler and Co. of Leeds – were relatively common in Essex. According to steam engine expert David Collidge the original rear wheels of this tractor have been removed, perhaps for maintenance, and replaced with a pair borrowed from the second engine in the background. Notice the detailed rendering of machine parts and the folds of cloth draped protectively over the body.

The countryside was changing, albeit slowly, and Ravilious was not alone in seeking to preserve evidence of the past. He met another devout chronicler of rural change in 1931, in rather strange circumstances. As Edward Bawden later described it, 'When Ravilious and I came down to the kitchen at Brick House to wash ourselves we found a stranger, stripped to the waist, pumping water over his head and making quite a splash in the large slate sink. He was tall, thin with black beady eyes rather close set, dark slightly curly hair, and as he greeted us his voice had a deep booming parsonic ring...'

This was Thomas Hennell, a parson's son who was himself a lay preacher. Hennell was on a cycling tour, gathering material for his book, *Change in the Farm* – eventually published in 1934 – and had taken a room with the retired stewardess. His heavy old army bicycle stood outside, a corn dollie tied firmly to the bar. Though rather awed by his classical bearing Ravilious and Bawden befriended him, and in 1935 he asked Ravilious to make four wood engravings to accompany his *Poems*, which were duly published the following year.

During the war, Hennell applied repeatedly to become a War Artist until, in 1943, he was commissioned and sent to Iceland to replace Ravilious. There he painted a number of fluent, breezy sketches before leaving to join the Allied invasion force on D-Day. He then moved on to India and Burma, only to be captured by terrorists in Indonesia in November 1945, and presumably killed. A devoted friend, Tom Hennell shared with Ravilious both a taste for melancholy dereliction and a tremendous sense of fun. After the last peacetime Christmas, Ravilious reported that 'Thomas Hennell who was here made a family sledge for six that rumbles as it goes and leaves tracks you can see on the Sudbury hill for miles away.'

Tractor, 1933, watercolour, 38.7 x 46.8 cm, Birmingham Museums and Art Gallery.

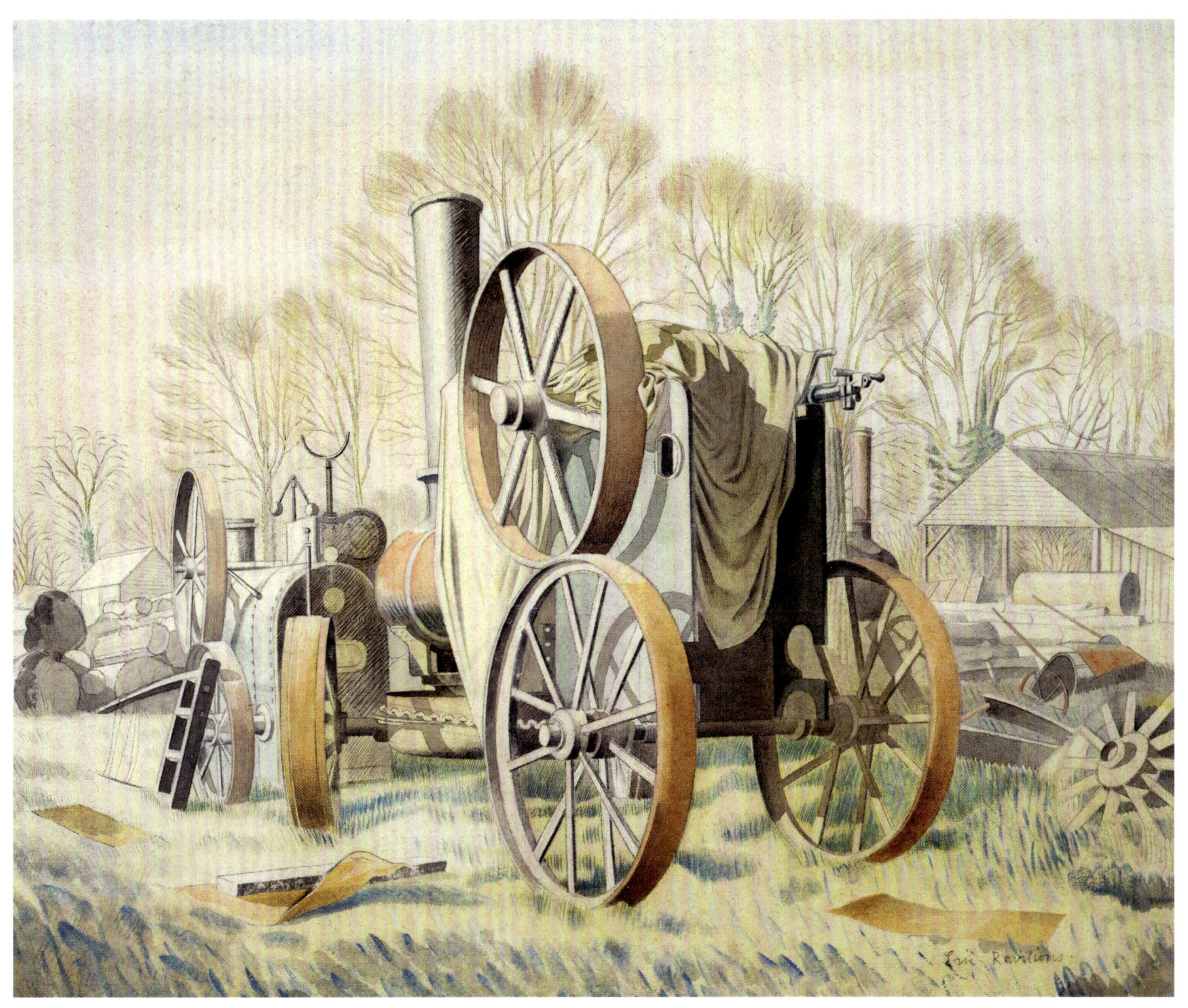

GARDEN PATH

On November 24, 1933, the Zwemmer Gallery in London launched an exhibition of Water-Colour Drawings by Eric Ravilious. This was his first solo show – Bawden's first was held a month earlier, at the same gallery – and the results were encouraging, with 20 of the 37 paintings sold. It also marked a transition in the artist's life, as the following year he and Tirzah set about finding their own house; perhaps this explains the slightly elegiac tone of this painting. Here are the same distinctive trees as appear in 'Prospect from an Attic', and the same shed, but the doors are closed now and the trees are leafless. In this context the white trelliswork gazebo – a wedding present from Ravilious and Tirzah to the Bawdens – appears as a reminder of summer and outdoor living.

According to Bliss there was a rift between the couples caused by an excess of Queen of Puddings – the only pudding, he claimed, that Tirzah knew how to make. More significant, no doubt, was Charlotte's pregnancy. Tirzah and Eric needed a place of their own, and with a new tenant found for their London flat they began frantically house-hunting. Finding nothing around Great Bardfield they looked in the vicinity of Furlongs, the Sussex cottage rented by Peggy Angus, where they discovered a pair of 19th-century caravans and converted them for use as a temporary home.

Finally, in September, Bawden found them a house in Castle Hedingham, a village nine miles from Great Bardfield. Named after a branch of Barclays which occupied part of the building, Bank House was owned by local grocer and haberdasher Henry Baines. Some years earlier his two children had contracted typhoid and he had bought the house to use as an isolation unit, manned by two specialist nurses from London.

Ravilious did not always see eye to eye with Baines, nicknaming him 'the old perisher', but he and Tirzah liked the house and took it, spending the autumn dealing with 'the business of leases – wallpapering – geysers and the rest of it'. There were no decorative excesses at Bank House, but a sober scheme of plain colour-washed walls and white paint, enlivened by Tirzah's marbled wallpapers. In the dining room visitors found a lithograph of 'Midnight Race on the Mississippi' with its twin-funnelled paddle steamers, and a collection of china carpet bowls.

'So far Edward has been the only visitor,' Ravilious wrote in December. 'He was mildly approving of everything and left early, promising to paper the hall as a Xmas present with a 4" map of Essex: but I am doing my best to stop this idea, not being very good at maps. The expense would be heavy too. We should be compelled to give the Bawdens a motor lawn mower at least.'

Garden Path, 1934, watercolour, 42 x 59 cm, Towner Art Gallery, Eastbourne.

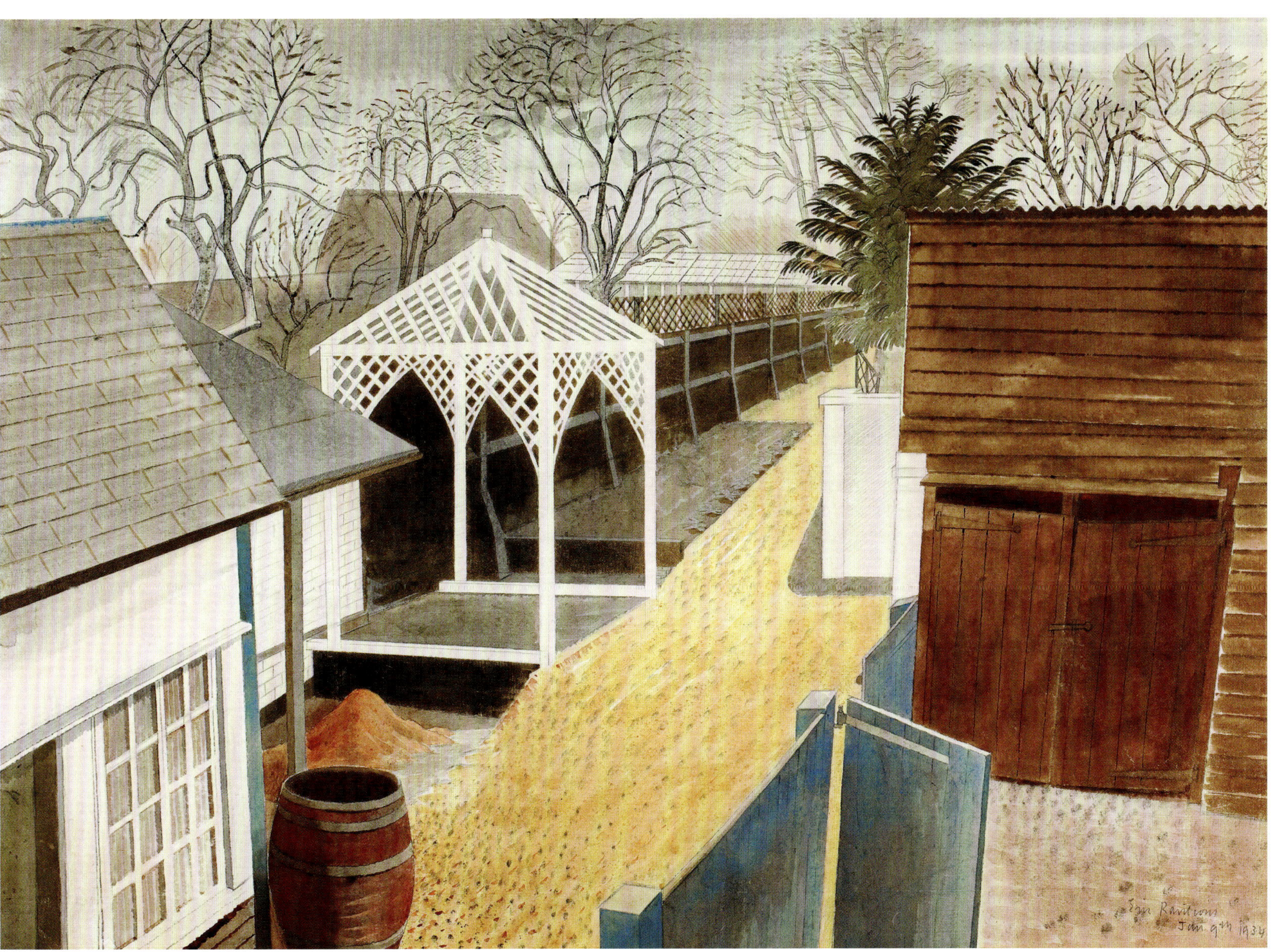

Asked in later years for a biographical sketch, Ravilious noted his 'tendency to paint in sequences (groups of broken down tractors and old cars and buses in fields, the discarded machinery of Essex)'. Here, an antique double-decker faces the sunlit, open countryside, as if about to drive away, yet it is only the shell or skeleton of a bus, standing not on wheels but on four barrels. With its tapering, top-heavy wooden body it could be an eccentric river boat, awaiting a rising tide. The number '29' has been painted on a folded piece of canvas or cardboard and wedged behind the staircase, perhaps as an aid to identification for potential buyers.

This is probably a view looking away from the 'repair yard for steam engines' that Tirzah later recalled, where Ravilious also discovered the subjects for 'Talbot-Darracq' and 'Tractor'. Engineer and blacksmith John Thomas Chapman began repairing steam engines and other agricultural machinery in 1870 at a yard on Bell Lane, Great Bardfield and the business was still going in the 1930s; the bungalows of Durham Close now occupy the site.

Tirzah noted that some of the engines were in working order, 'Though the bindweed was climbing over them and there was a hen's nest in one. The door of the shed where they repaired wheels was splashed with a variety of paints and inside were some lovely red wheels.

'Eric was very excited with the yard,' she remarked, 'and set to work drawing the engines and the car, afterwards tinting in watercolour his very careful drawings.'

But why is this bus here, in a country junkyard? It looks like a city vehicle, a double-decker with the distinctive curved stairway of the B-type London buses built by the London General Omnibus Company in Walthamstow before and during World War I. Hundreds of these vehicles were used as ambulances and troop transports on the Western Front, their bodywork painted khaki and windows replaced by wooden panels. After the war some returned to service in the capital, but were quickly replaced by newer models and dispatched to the provinces, until the passage of time caught up with them even in rural districts. Eventually it became quite common to see a B-type bus dismantled in this way, its cab and chassis perhaps put to use in haulage while the body waits to be transformed into a henhouse, shed or, possibly, somebody's home.

Following the move to Castle Hedingham Ravilious soon found a new junkyard, where he painted a hansom cab, and which he described as 'an area wholly mud given up to every sort of junk, beds and bicycles and cartwheels with ducks and hens and black-faced enormous sheep to liven the scene...

'These brutes,' he added, 'run about the place jumping pans and corrugated iron with a beautiful agility and a great deal of clatter.'

No. 29 Bus, 1934, watercolour, 45 x 55 cm, Towner Art Gallery, Eastbourne.

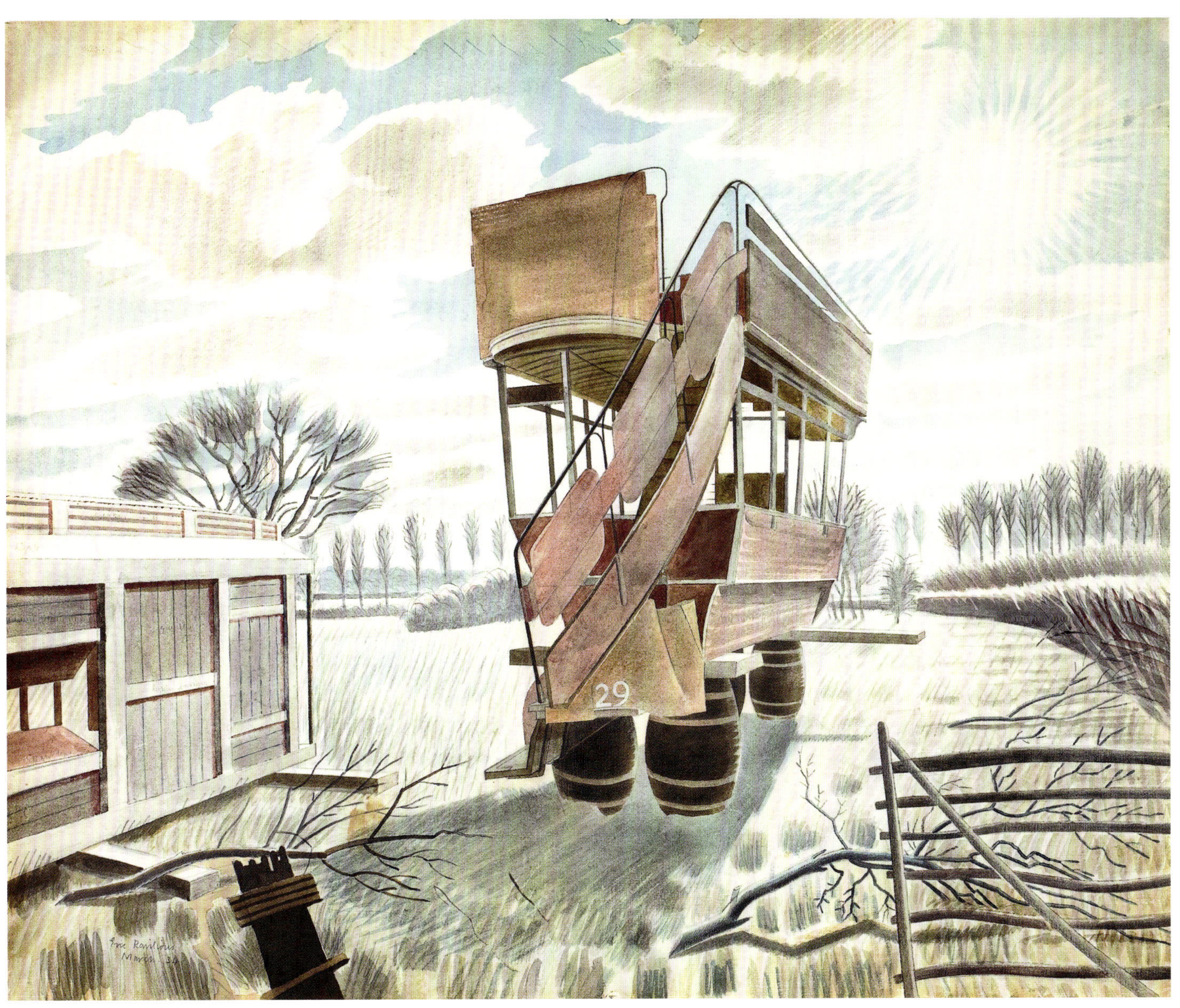

29

BACK GARDENS

Although Ravilious endured many discomforts for his art, wet weather forced him indoors, and he chose this scene partly because it could be painted from an upstairs window of Bank House. He had recently been to Newman's of Soho Square, London – an artist's colourman that had been grinding and mixing paints for a century at least – and had a new colour to try.

'I would have drawn this afternoon out of the window upstairs if it had rained,' he noted in March 1935, 'and spent most of the morning preparing for it – now the weather has cleared a bit, so I've not been able to try out the brown madder for the wet roofs and garden walls in this drawing...'

The rain evidently returned. Beneath dark clouds, the keep of Hedingham Castle stands on the wooded hilltop, the leafless branches and general gloom giving it a remote, ominous air. With this as a backdrop the arched gateway frames a moment of everyday drama, as the coalman enters through it, bent under the weight of the sack on his back.

One of the artist's favourite pastimes was to visit the cinema in neighbouring Sible Hedingham, where he was particularly attracted to the charms of the 'incomparable' Ginger Rogers. He was also a fan of Alfred Hitchcock, and in this painting the blank window and crazy drainpipe, the castle surrounded by leafless trees and the dark figure in the foreground all conspire to create an unsettling atmosphere. Yet this is at the same time simply a view over the back gardens of an English village that dates back to Domesday.

Construction of the castle itself was begun in the 12th century by Aubrey de Vere, whose father fought alongside William the Conqueror at the Battle of Hastings and was repaid with a vast gift of Saxon lands. Aubrey was killed in a London riot in 1141, but his son, Aubrey III, continued the work. A warrior like his predecessors, Aubrey III was made Earl of Oxford, cementing the family's place in medieval history, and the de Veres' prestige ensured that the castle remained in the family until 1728. Through marriage it passed into the Majendie family, and it was Mrs Majendie whom Ravilious approached in March 1935 with a request to sketch within the castle grounds.

A few weeks later the villagers were there en masse, celebrating the Silver Jubilee of George V with sports and a torchlight procession and bonfires. They had decorated the village with such enthusiasm that when Ravilious went to buy triangular pennons he found they were sold out, so Tirzah made some out of shirting and yellow satin. These were stretched all around the railings in front of Bank House, making at night, Ravilious noted, 'a curious rustling noise'.

Back Gardens, 1935, watercolour, 48.2 x 61 cm, private collection.

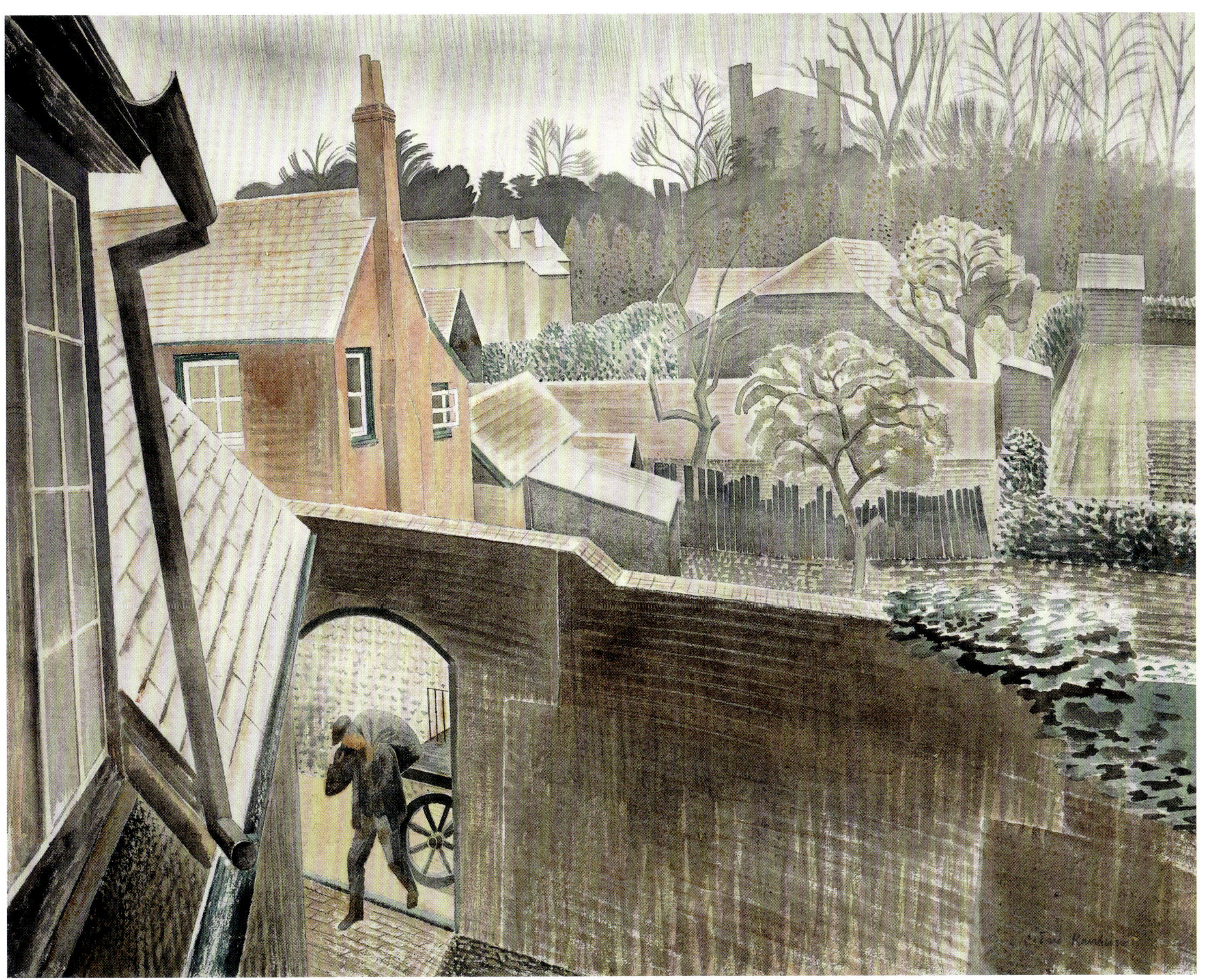

FRIESIAN BULL

Hoof-deep in mud, framed by high, many-windowed walls, a bull stands chained by the nose, his black head turned towards us, eyes closed like an imprisoned king contemplating his next move. This is another of the artist's disquieting paintings, in which the lightness of the medium balances the mythic weight of the subject matter: a great bull chained within ancient walls.

By 1935 Ravilious was in great demand as a wood engraver. Most mornings the post brought a commission from the Curwen Press, London Transport or another regular employer, and he would then spend the day at his worktable in the large bay window at Bank House. A couple of years earlier Mary Branson had enjoyed watching him at work, and described him sitting 'by the window with his wood-cutting block of boxwood and a leather cushion under it – turning it this way and that as he went on cutting, and whistling all the time as beautifully as any bird – always on the in-breath, never the out'.

Whenever his busy and unpredictable work schedule allowed, however, Ravilious left his studio and went off on foot or by bicycle to paint. After the success of his first solo show, the Zwemmer Gallery was planning to hold a second exhibition in 1936, and Ravilious searched far and wide for new, inspiring subjects. The small farms in the vicinity were a rich source of material, although only a few paintings survived his ruthless quality control. Chickens he painted, and pigs, animals about which he loved everything 'except the eye'.

On one occasion he arrived at a piggery to find the animals subdued, having just been gelded. 'I am thankful to say,' he wrote, 'I arrived just after the 38th and last pig was finished. The gelder,' he added, 'was a nice old man. He told me he gets 4d a pig and does nothing but visit piggeries...'

Ravilious found this bull penned in a magnificent barn at the Great Lodge, a mile from Great Bardfield. One of Tom Hennell's favourite buildings, the barn was constructed around 1540 for Anne of Cleves, after Henry VIII gave her the Bardfield estate as part of their divorce settlement. The estate itself is far older, and is listed as a manor in the Domesday Book, but this barn is the longest-surviving building, its solid walls and loop windows echoing the architecture of a medieval castle. Grade 1 listed, it is still standing today, the lowest tier of windows blocked up as they are in this painting.

The bull too is intriguing, one of a small number of pedigree Friesian cattle imported from Holland in the first half of the 20th century. Today Friesians produce most of our milk, but in 1935 bulls like this were a comparative rarity – bovine royalty.

Friesian Bull, 1935, watercolour, 46 x 56 cm, private collection.

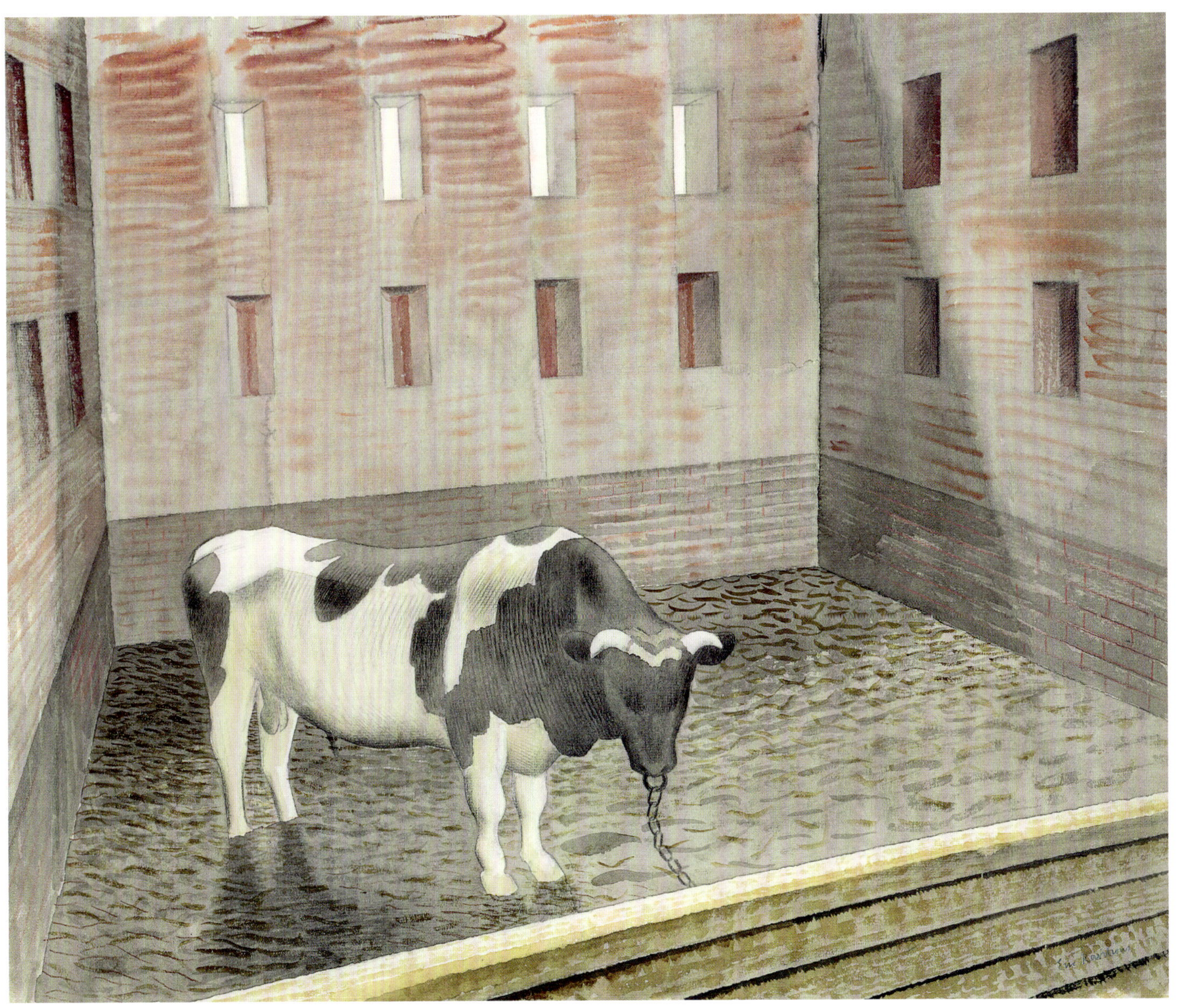

THE BRICKYARD

As he continued to assemble paintings for his second solo show, Ravilious sought out what he called 'surprising places'. He sketched in an industrial sandpit, where sand martins nested in the cliffs, and in a coalyard, and in this strange old brickyard. The steam engine and associated machinery seem to belong in the Victorian age, yet this was a working industrial site when Ravilious discovered it, two years after Adolf Hitler's accession to power.

The Roman bricks incorporated into the fabric of St Peter's church, Sible Hedingham, testify to the importance of brickmaking in the area. With no stone to quarry, builders relied on bricks made from local deposits of London Clay. With the opening of the Colne Valley and Halstead Railway in the early 1860s production expanded so that, by the turn of the century, Hedingham yards were producing more than 10 million bricks a year, and exporting them not only to London but also to Ireland and as far as Egypt.

At its peak the Hedingham Brick Company and other businesses employed 500 men, and despite a subsequent decline there were still six family-owned brickyards operating in 1935. Of these all but one have closed, but the Bulmer Brick and Tile Company survived until a new enthusiasm for restoring Victorian buildings – most famously, perhaps, London's St Pancras Station – created a market for old-fashioned, handmade bricks.

The brickyard shown here is not Bulmer. However, thanks to detective work by local historian Adrian Corder-Birch, we do know which of the other five sites it is. He found the vital clue in an auction catalogue from November 1938, which lists the plant and effects of the Tortoise Brick Works. Item 97 reads '8 hp portable engine by Garrett, double shafts and belting', and item 99, 'Erection of wash-mill, 3 pulleys, crown-wheel, shafting, etc complete.' The steam engine shown here matches the description in the catalogue, and the low hill in the background also fits; it lies behind the site of the Tortoise works, on Wethersfield Road, Sible Hedingham.

Eli Cornish set up the business in 1886, installing the steam engine and wash mill that were still in use when he passed it on to his son, Captain Fred Cornish, in 1931. Seven years later the Tortoise Brick Works closed, the machinery was auctioned off, and the site with its man-made pits and mounds became overgrown. But Tortoise House, which Eli built, still stands beside the former works, and other evidence also survives. The Tortoise Brick Works made over a hundred different types of red brick, as well as a range of moulded, ornamental and arch bricks, of which many examples can still be seen today around the Hedinghams.

Detective work has also been carried out on the painting itself. The Ashmolean Museum reported in 1968, 'The sheet has been patched by the artist to cover a hand-barrow in the foreground.'

The Brickyard, 1935, watercolour, 48.7 x 56.8 cm, Ashmolean Museum, Oxford.

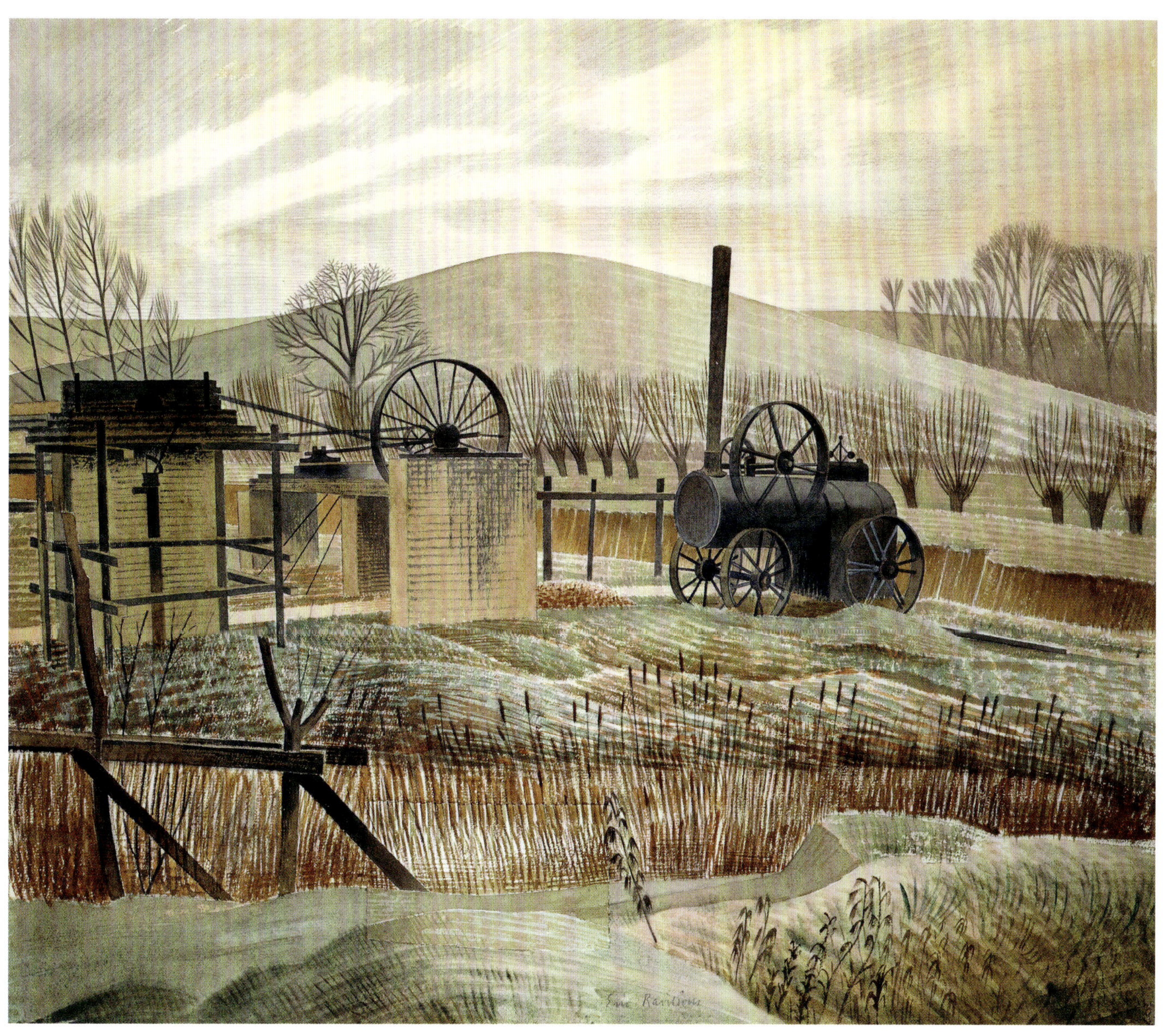

HULL'S MILL

There is no mystery about the subject of this painting. Hull's Mill is a much-loved Hedingham landmark, a watermill built in 1848 on a site used for milling since Domesday and probably earlier. Ravilious was enchanted by 'this extraordinarily attractive place', which was also known in the 1930s as the Hovis Mill in reference to its owner, Hovis Ltd, and after discovering it in May 1935 returned many times. On 2 June he wrote to Helen Binyon:

'I want to go out again this evening to a Hovis mill — rather like the one at Barcombe and pretty as possible, white and almost new looking; there is one of those shallow streams in the foreground (of the drawing I've begun) that goes across the road — a pleasure to cycle through it and makes such a pleasant gurgling noise.'

If this is the drawing in question he succeeded in tempering the prettiness of the building; the open upstairs window and the dark doorway filled with stacked sacks add a frisson of mystery. As well as making a wood engraving for a brochure advertising Green Line Buses for London Transport, Ravilious started at least three drawings of the building, one of which had some help from the weather later in the month:

'It rained heavily this morning and covered the drawing (the same old mill) with speckles, which seemed a pity at the time but now I rather like. The woman at the house there lent me a nursing chair with the legs sawn off as I'd forgotten to bring a stool — and I had not brought water either so used the millstream. Anyhow it soon rained too hard for these things to matter.'

His forgetfulness is understandable, since Tirzah was only days away from giving birth to their first child. John Ravilious was born on 21 June at the hospital in Halstead, an institution that impressed the new father. 'They produce tea at every visit and any hour and actually offer cigarettes,' he reported enthusiastically. 'I didn't know hospitals were ever like this.'

With bus services generally unreliable and almost non-existent on Sundays, Ravilious spent the weeks after his son's birth cycling here, there and everywhere. One Sunday he reported riding from Halstead with a suitcase, after a lunch of steak and kidney pie and ice cream — 'so am feeling hot but virtuous'.

On another occasion he had a punctured tyre en route to the mill, 'and deciding it was time for a new one, rode home on a flat tyre for three miles, uphill work but rather fun. The noise of the valve bumping intermittently was like a train — sort of bum-bump-caballum of a noise that tinkled the bell, and surprised everyone on the road. They looked round to see what was coming.'

Hull's Mill, 1935, watercolour, 45 x 55 cm, Fry Art Gallery, Saffron Walden.

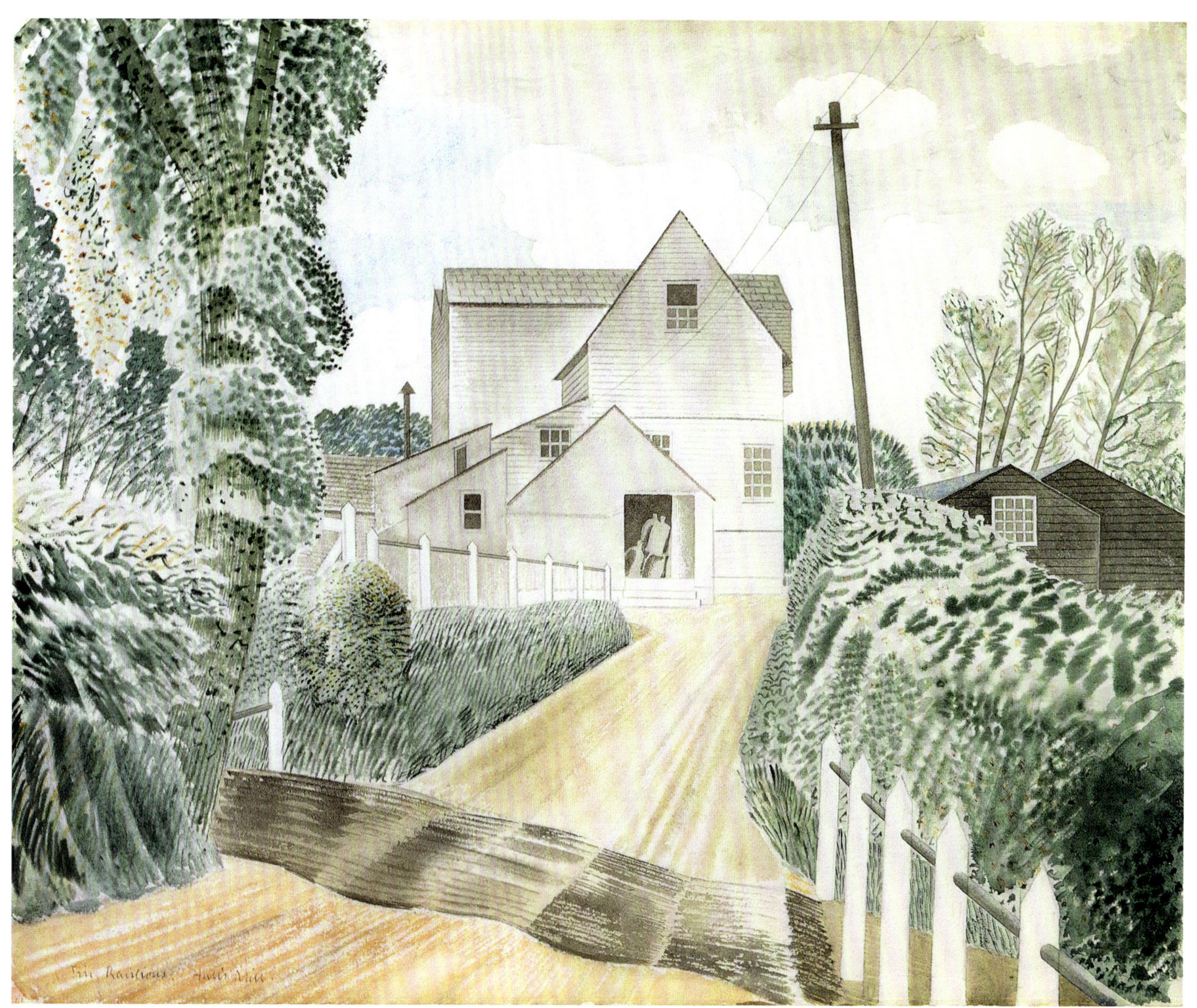

BUTCHER'S SHOP

A butcher stands at his block, handling a joint of meat. A pig's head lies to one side, while on hooks at the window are displayed an array of other joints, alongside rabbits and a pheasant. A pair of scales and assorted weights lie on a counter to the right, and above it sheets of newspaper hang on a hook, ready for wrapping. One can imagine the satisfying weight of a pound of chops wrapped in paper.

'I've been drawing the butcher's shop and enjoying it rather,' Ravilious wrote the autumn after John's birth. 'The sawdust gets into things and there is very little room to work in this box of a place but the meat and rabbits and pigeons are very nice to draw…'

Evidently he was inspired by the subject, but we might still wonder why an artist with a burgeoning reputation as a painter of thoughtful, idiosyncratic landscapes should be drawing the interior of a butcher's shop. The answer lies in his relationship with the Golden Cockerel Press, the publishing house whose owner Robert Gibbings had helped Ravilious establish his reputation as a wood engraver in the late 1920s. Having illustrated a number of books for the press, most recently *The Hansom Cab and the Pigeons* (1935), Ravilious asked Golden Cockerel to consider a book based on an alphabet of shops, and in July 1935 they agreed.

As a shopkeeper's son, the subject was one Ravilious knew and loved, and he selected shops with a connoisseur's eye. However, his determination to illustrate the book using autolithography rather than wood engraving made the financial risk too great for Golden Cockerel, and they decided not to proceed; he therefore approached Country Life Books, where publisher Noel Carrington was pioneering children's books illustrated using the medium Ravilious preferred. In 1938 Country Life duly published *High Street* as a book for children, with 24 exquisite illustrations and text by J. M. Richards, an architectural writer and old friend of Eric's.

'There are about thirty-two yards of gut in a pig,' he tells us in the essay on the Family Butcher. 'There is about the same amount in a sheep, but the sheep's gut is chiefly used for making the strings of tennis racquets.'

The accompanying illustration shows not this interior but an exterior view, although it is clear from the design of the window that the shop is the same. This we know – thanks to research by Adrian Corder-Birch – was Newman's of Sible Hedingham, a business set up in 1912 by Mark Newman. It traded until 1989, when Mark's son Douglas Gordon Newman retired. Thereafter the premises were used as an antique shop, then a smokehouse selling fish and game. It is now home to Elite Hair Design, where you can lie on a sunbed in a back room that still has meat hooks hidden above the ceiling.

Butcher's Shop, 1935, watercolour, 48 x 58.5 cm, Towner Art Gallery, Eastbourne.

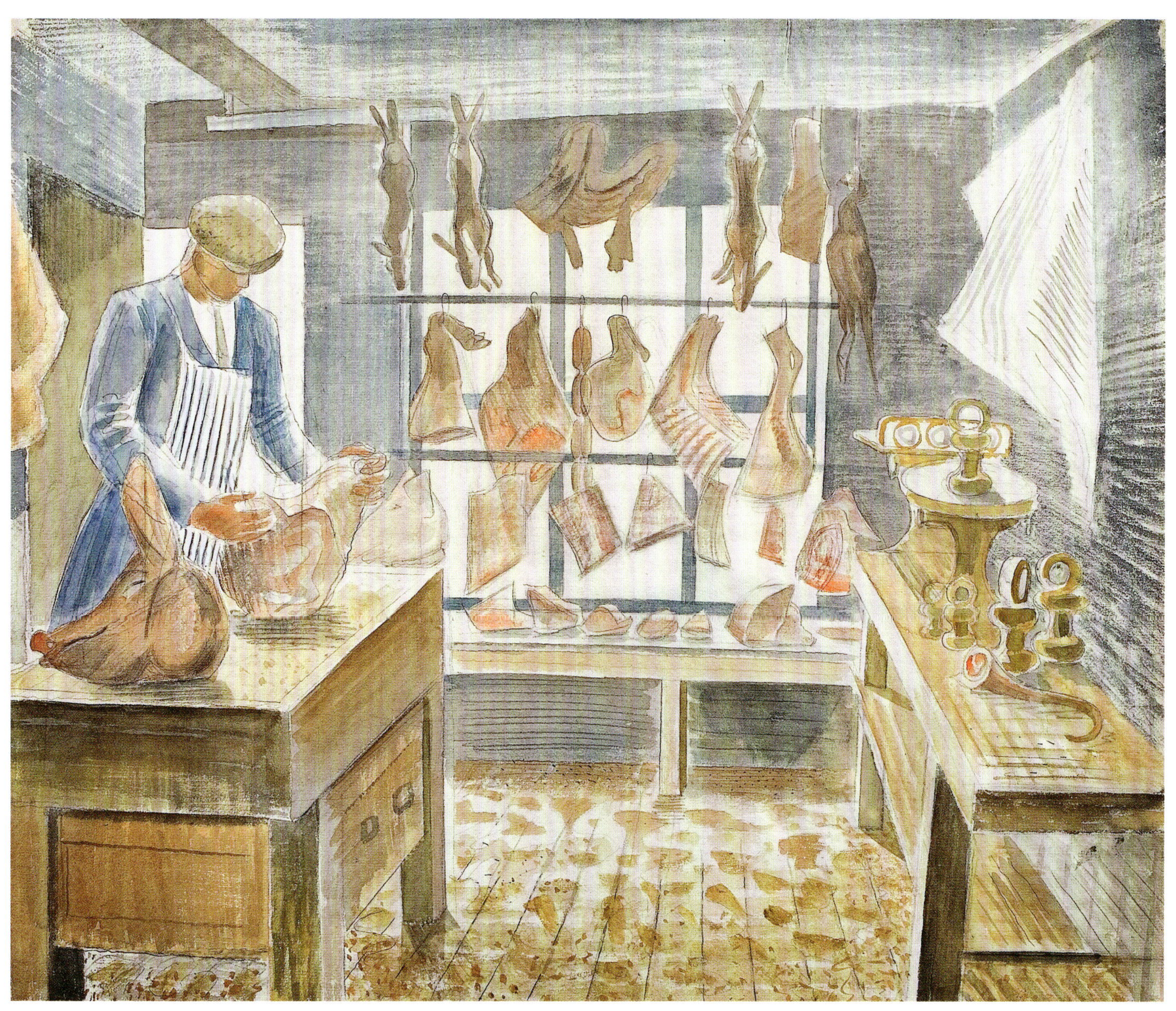

TRAIN GOING OVER A BRIDGE AT NIGHT

A passenger train, blazing with light, crosses a bridge over a country lane, illuminating the dark village for a few moments as a magnificent plume of smoke billows from the funnel. Ravilious was a train traveller both by inclination and by necessity, and in his 1939 painting 'Train Landscape' he recreated the interior of a compartment in tantalising detail; here he offers a different, but equally compelling vision. If J. M. W. Turner's 1844 painting 'Rain, Steam and Speed' portrayed the locomotive as a dark and elemental presence, this watercolour shows a train that is bright, modern and amiable, like a toy.

The building of the Colne Valley and Halstead Railway in the early 1860s had a dramatic effect on life in the Hedinghams, encouraging the expansion of industries that could export manufactured goods cheaply and easily. At the same time the railway system brought the countryside suddenly closer to the cities. While this hastened the movement of working people from country to town, it also encouraged the emigration of those willing to commute to work. London's artistic and literary community scattered around the Home Counties.

In the 1930s four trains ran daily (two on Sundays) in each direction from Sible and Castle Hedingham Station, just off to the left of this picture, connecting with services on the main lines that linked the capital to Cambridge and Norwich. This suited Ravilious perfectly, since he needed to travel regularly to London to teach and never learned to drive.

Other newcomers were also attracted by the Hedingham rail service, and two years after Eric and Tirzah's arrival another young couple moved into High House, just down the road. Robert Goodden ran a design business while Kay had read English at Somerville College, Oxford. As an avid reader – P. G. Wodehouse for fun, H. G. Wells or Boswell for something more serious – Ravilious was delighted to meet Kay, and the four took to spending evenings together playing dominoes or visiting the cinema in Sible Hedingham. At the height of the Spanish Civil War, when political tensions were running high, Ravilious wrote to Helen Binyon, 'The Gooddens have a vicious game (strong capitalist interests) called Monopoly...'

By this time the railway was already beginning to lose business, as people increasingly took to the roads, and by 1965 the Colne Valley line was closed and dismantled. One can still catch a train from Sible and Castle Hedingham Station, however, thanks to the local rail enthusiasts who, a decade later, began to rebuild a mile-long stretch of track to the north-west of Castle Hedingham. They then took the abandoned station apart brick by brick, transported it a mile, and reassembled it beside the new line. Today, the Colne Valley Railway is more popular than ever, proving that Ravilious was not alone in his affection for trains.

Train Going over a Bridge at Night, 1935, watercolour, 40 x 50 cm, private collection.

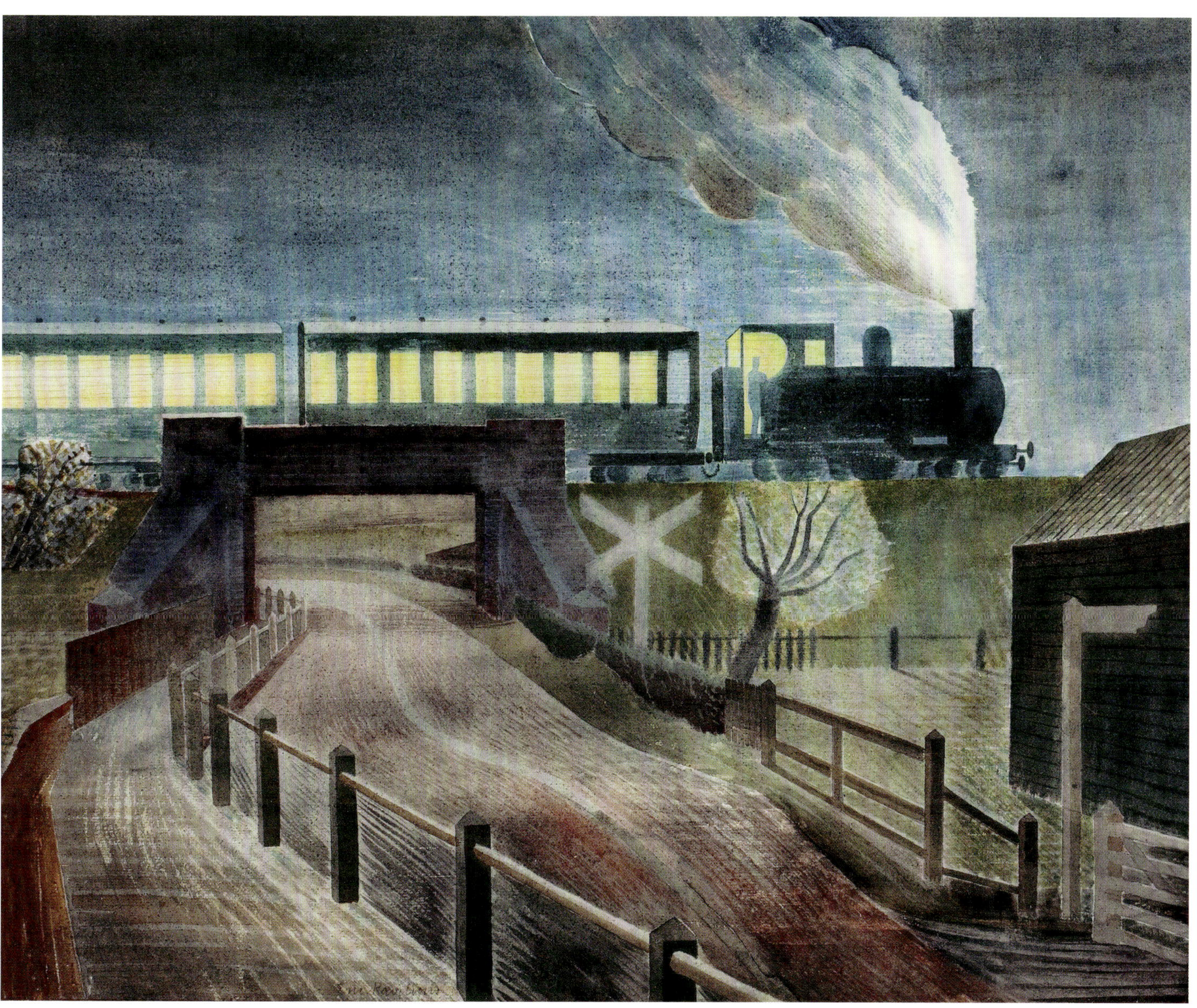

HALSTEAD ROAD IN SNOW

Tyre tracks disappear down a snow-covered lane, beside an elegant Georgian house, as if the people who made them were here just a moment ago. We are in Castle Hedingham, at the junction of Queen Street and Sheepcot Road – also known as Halstead Road – and snow is falling, large flakes covering the picture surface and pulling the eye this way and that. Ravilious was fascinated by winter, relishing the light and colours peculiar to the season, and on this occasion he hurried over breakfast so as not to miss a morning snow shower, starting a drawing outside and then finishing it in his studio.

'Scratching the spots all over the drawing later with a penknife was a change,' he wrote to Helen Binyon, 'and I enjoyed it. I have in mind a series of drawings of houses in this village because in winter they are such a lovely colour.'

He was fortunate to live in a village with numerous fine old houses – over 100 are listed – lining the streets around the 12th-century church of St Nicholas, many of them displaying the decorative brickwork that is such a distinctive local feature. Sheepcot House, which can be seen behind the tree in this painting, was built during Shakespeare's lifetime, and was the birthplace in 1682 of naturalist Mark Catesby, who later published and illustrated the first account of the flora and fauna of Britain's American colonies.

Today the horse chestnut tree still stands on Chapel Green, as the patch of grass at the junction is known, but the lanes are not so quiet. The tracks shown here – loose, flowing lines in contrast to the hard geometry of the buildings – were made by bicycles and prams, and they remind us that pre-war Castle Hedingham was a predominantly pedestrian settlement. Local shops catered to most needs, while coal, bread and milk were delivered.

On one occasion Ravilious wrote, 'The milkman made me laugh today. We write up any money owing on the side of the door, and I asked if we owed tenpence. He put his head in and said, "Yes, the writing's on the wall."'

And then there was the postman, on whom Ravilious relied almost totally for communication with the world outside the village. With telephones still comparatively rare and unreliable, all arrangements, commissions and payments were made by post, and waiting for the postman was a national pastime.

'I woke up with a feeling that I wouldn't sleep any more and might as well get up,' Ravilious reported one winter morning, 'and saw the aged postman down the street. He took his time of course – he has a zigzag course and a shuffle that has all time before it – and until each letter has been looked at carefully with a lamp you don't get it.'

Halstead Road in Snow, 1935, watercolour, 45 x 56 cm, private collection.

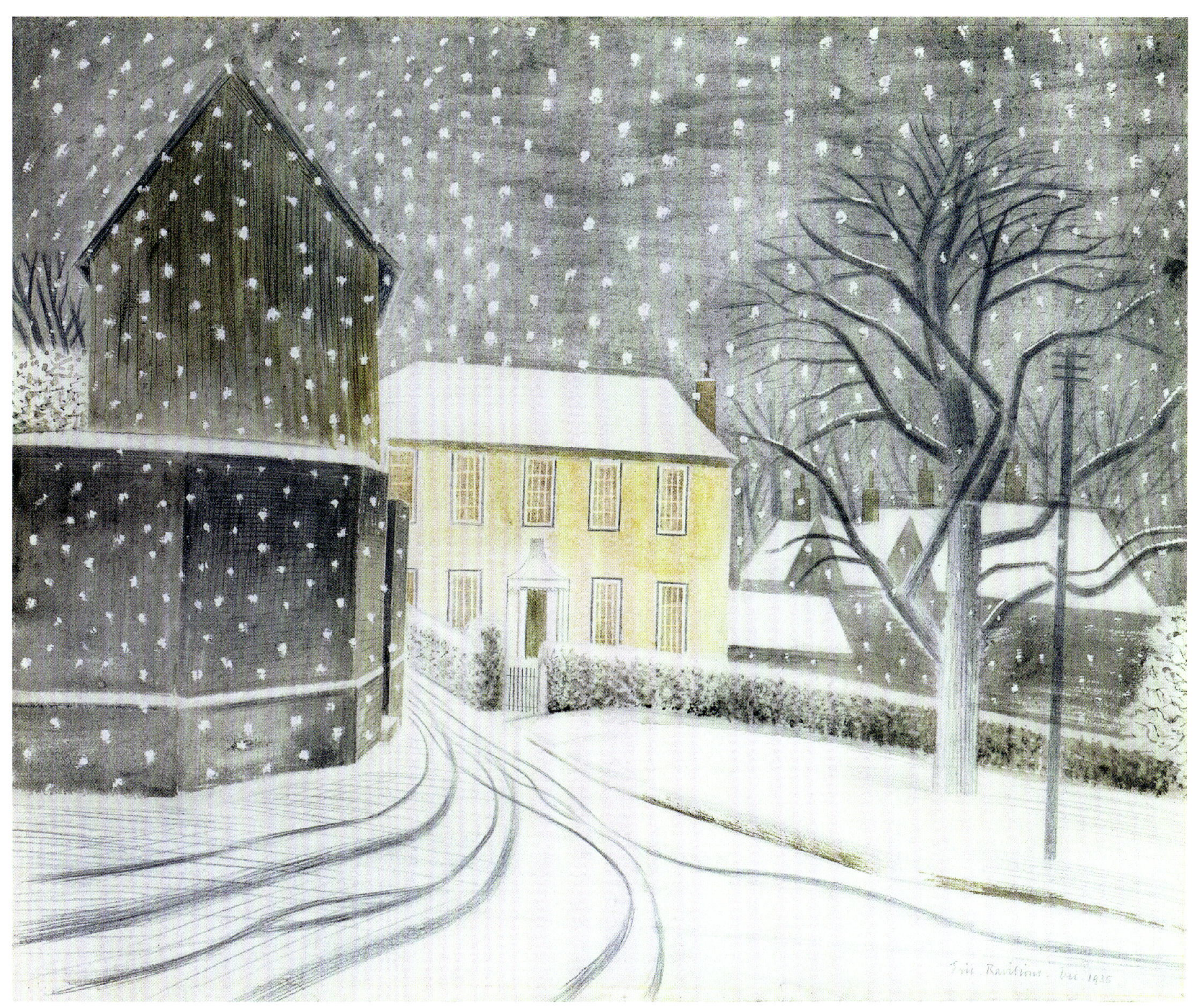

VICARAGE

The creeper rampant on the walls, the radiant light and the figure at the gate suggest a warm season, but the bare tree almost hidden in the background tells us that it is winter, in fact 25th December. 'The usual green Christmas here,' Ravilious noted at the time.

He had already painted the splendid Georgian house once that year, in the January snow, but barely knew the vicar. The following year, however, a new vicar was appointed, and when Ravilious went to introduce himself he was delighted to find him tending a bonfire of his predecessor's temperance hymn books. Guy and Evelyn Hepher became great friends of Ravilious and Tirzah, and their son David a playmate for John.

'This letter will be a bit wobbly,' Ravilious wrote in July 1936, 'through playing tennis so much this morning – my first game for years – it was spirited but erratic play. The vicar's service is deadly.'

Guy Hepher was both curious and creative. On one occasion he became convinced that a mural lay hidden behind the plaster inside the church, and on another Ravilious found him drawing out a plan of the church in seven colours. Not long after moving in, he asked the artist to look over the old church records and maps with him.

'There are some fine names and quantities of the most beautiful handwriting,' Ravilious reported. 'I liked Zorababel Ginn, and I liked the Bastardy book. You wouldn't think in a quiet village like this there had been so much guilty passion...'

This painting also serves as a kind of record. The woman at the gate is Mrs Lizzie Sams (née Slaughter), who lived with her husband Alfred in Trinity Cottage, to the right of the picture; both worked at Trinity Hall, another fine 18th-century building which can be glimpsed to the left of the vicarage. Lizzie is evidently waiting for the baker's boy, whose cart stands in the foreground. Ravilious saw this cart often from the bay window of Bank House, and painted it at least twice; here the spoked wooden wheels and tapering handles are meticulously drawn, with the bread itself visible within.

The vicarage is no more than a backdrop to this daily drama, but it would become a vital refuge for the Ravilious family during the brutally cold winters at the end of the decade.

'I like exceptional weather,' Ravilious wrote in January 1940, 'but it is making country life rather difficult – and we now live in the vicarage as Bank House is quite impossible... We go up on the roof periodically with brooms and shovels to clear the snow... What you can see of the village in plan is lovely, but it is very hard work. I throw an occasional snowball like a bomb at people like Miss Grant in the road.'

Vicarage, 1935, watercolour, 45 x 55.5 cm, private collection.

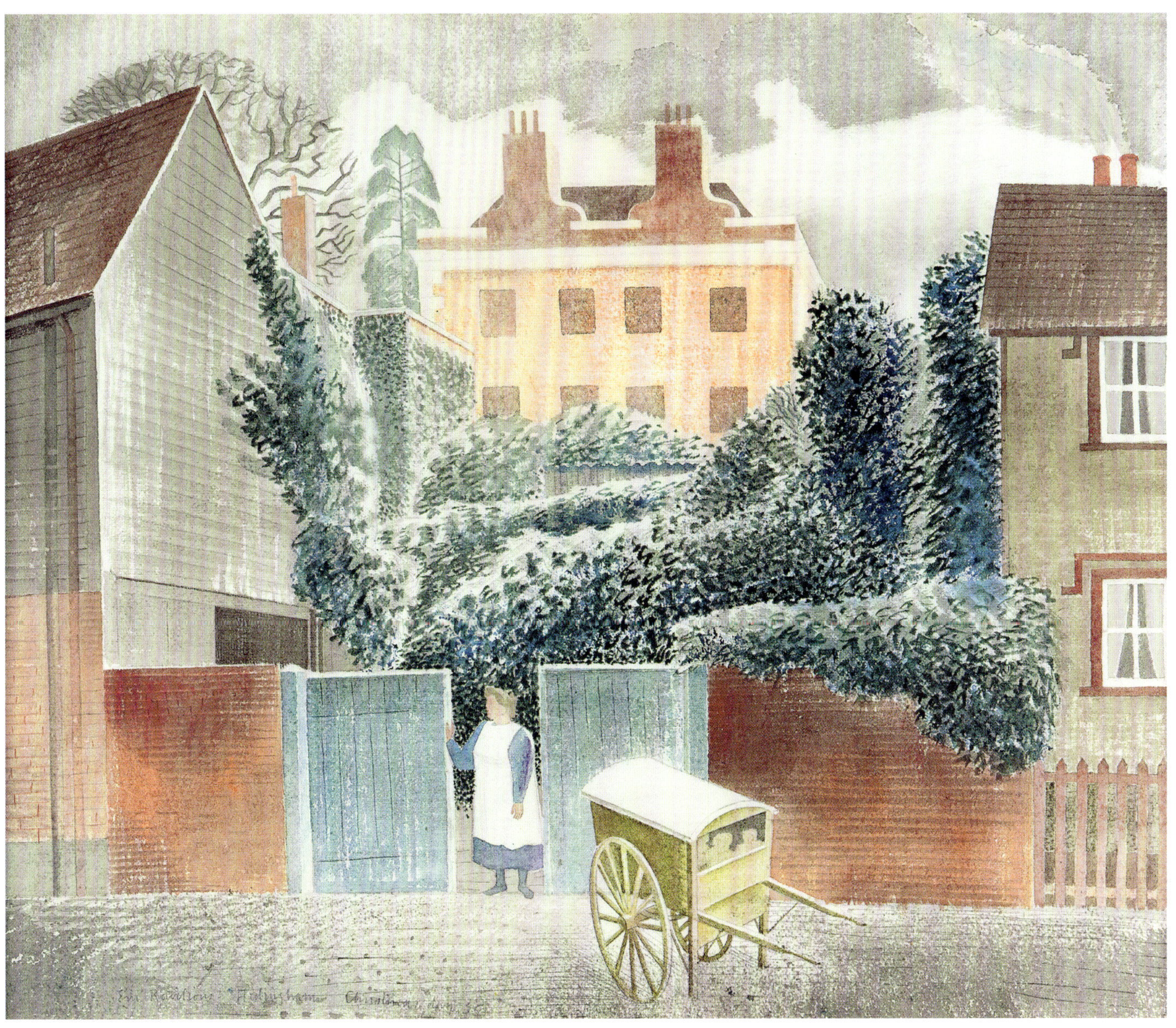

VILLAGE STREET

In February 1936 a second solo exhibition of watercolours by Eric Ravilious was held at the Zwemmer Gallery, London, and this time 28 paintings were sold out of 36 exhibited. For the rest of the year the artist turned away from painting and focused on design work, with a commission from Wedgwood for Edward VIII's coronation mug (amended after the abdication to celebrate the crowning of George VI) and continued demand for his wood engravings. His time was also increasingly taken up with the illustrations for *High Street*.

With no further exhibition of watercolours likely until 1939 one may wonder why he paused from his other labours to make this whimsical painting, which shows a man and a woman cycling through Falcon Square, Castle Hedingham, on a wet day. In the background stands Augusta House, another of the village's remarkable Georgian buildings and home to 'the old perisher'. Mr Baines's grocery and haberdashery business was evidently prospering, as were numerous other local shops.

Of these, two found their way into the pages of *High Street*: the saddlery next door to the Bell Inn, across the street from Bank House; and a hardware shop, which was identified recently from a photograph showing its owner, Bennett Smith, standing proudly in the doorway. Born the son of a Falcon Square shopkeeper in 1877, Smith trained locally

as a cabinet maker before setting up in business in the first decade of the 20th century. Later, while his brother Walter became Postmaster, Bennett opened a hardware store, which was still in business in 1950. Ravilious was very taken with the shop, which had chamber pots hanging from the ceiling and a distinctive smell of paraffin oil. It stood just to the right of this picture, while Mr and Mrs Smith lived next door, in the building shown.

In *High Street* the shop is depicted with a penny farthing bicycle displayed on the roof, a detail added to the composition by Ravilious from sketches made at a bicycle shop in the neighbouring market town of Sudbury. But why place an antique bike above a hardware shop? Perhaps it was a reference to Bennett Smith's favourite hobby, as he and his wife were keen cyclists, and used to ride off for a picnic on early closing day. According to contemporary accounts, this painting shows the couple setting off for an afternoon ride, but it also reminds us of a time when far more people rode bicycles than drove cars. Ravilious himself cycled everywhere, whether visiting friends or looking for subjects to paint, in all weathers.

'There have been great snow storms here,' he wrote one March, 'and we were badly caught in one cycling over to Bardfield yesterday and arrived like Shackleton and Scott late for tea and they had eaten all the hot cross buns.'

Village Street, 1936, watercolour, 40 x 52 cm, Towner Art Gallery, on loan from Eastbourne Sixth Form College.

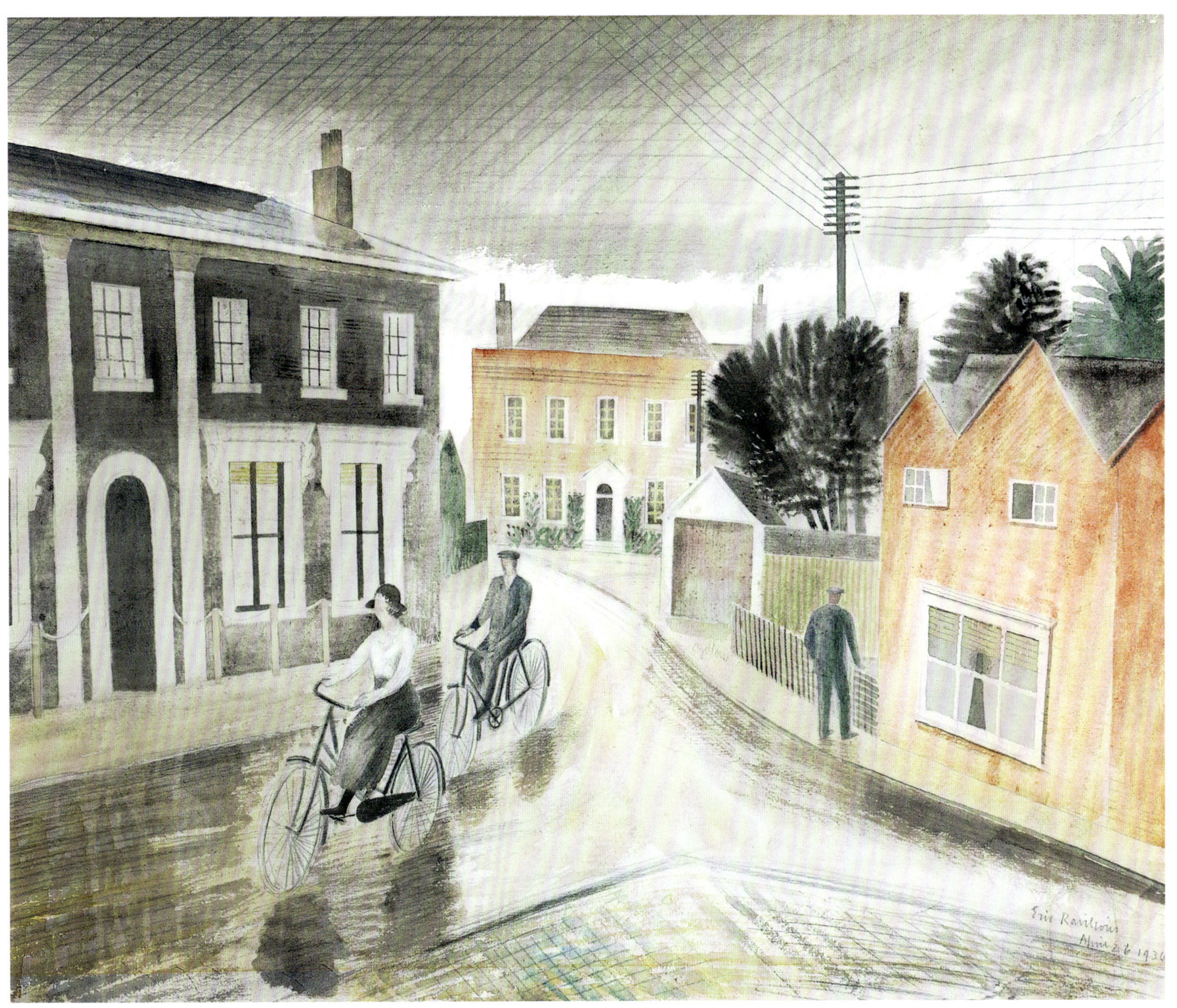

SALT MARSH

A wooden boat lies, apparently abandoned, on a desolate coast, surrounded by a formless expanse of mud. Lying on its side, timbers exposed where the decking is missing, the boat resembles the skeleton of some beached sea creature, an impression belied by the strong, sensual curve of the hull. The smaller boat tucked in, almost under the hull, lends this image a maternal quality; the larger boat, damaged though it may be, offers security in an otherwise inhospitable scene.

This vision has particular resonance in the circumstances of the time, with Hitler's aggressive stance towards Czechoslovakia threatening to escalate into war. Ravilious and Bawden were both actively involved in the Artists' International Association, which supported the Republican side in the Spanish Civil War through fund-raising exhibitions, commissions and other ventures, and Brick House had become something of a focal point for radical politics. Indeed, the attic room sketched by Ravilious was given over for a time to two refugees from the war in Spain, as Bawden described them, 'A Colonel and Major of the Republican army, in ordinary life a medical student walking the hospital and a barber from Seville.'

These were not the only refugees who found their way to Essex. By October 1938 the Hephers had a 12-year-old Jewish girl from Germany living with them, and not long afterwards the Gooddens took in a Polish woman who had spent two years in a concentration camp. Another Pole, Wolfgang Münser, stayed with the Ravilious family in 1939. This was nothing compared to the influx of evacuees from London at the outbreak of war, but it shows that events in Europe had an impact even in an Essex village.

Nevertheless, Ravilious was working hard, preparing for an exhibition the following year at the London gallery of Arthur Tooth and Sons. On this occasion he was staying at The King's Head in Tollesbury, a village just inland of the salt marshes bordering the River Blackwater. Between rainstorms he set out 'to draw boats and black and white warehouses and the Essex mud flats ... running for the tea hut over the ditches when the rain came down'.

One aim of such excursions was to find places and subjects that no one else had painted, so he was mildly perturbed to bump into Vivian Pitchforth, an artist he knew from the RCA. Pitchforth apparently introduced him to a companion as 'Ravilious who sells all his pictures', adding waspishly, in reference to a popular romantic novelist of the age, 'He and Bawden are a proper couple of Ethel M. Dells — only better aesthetically.'

Pitchforth later gave his own version of the meeting. 'I was living on a boat,' he recounted, 'and went on deck, bleary-eyed, to look at what God Almighty had to offer early in the morning, and there was Rav already at it.'

Salt Marsh, 1938, watercolour, 40.2 x 52.8 cm, private collection.

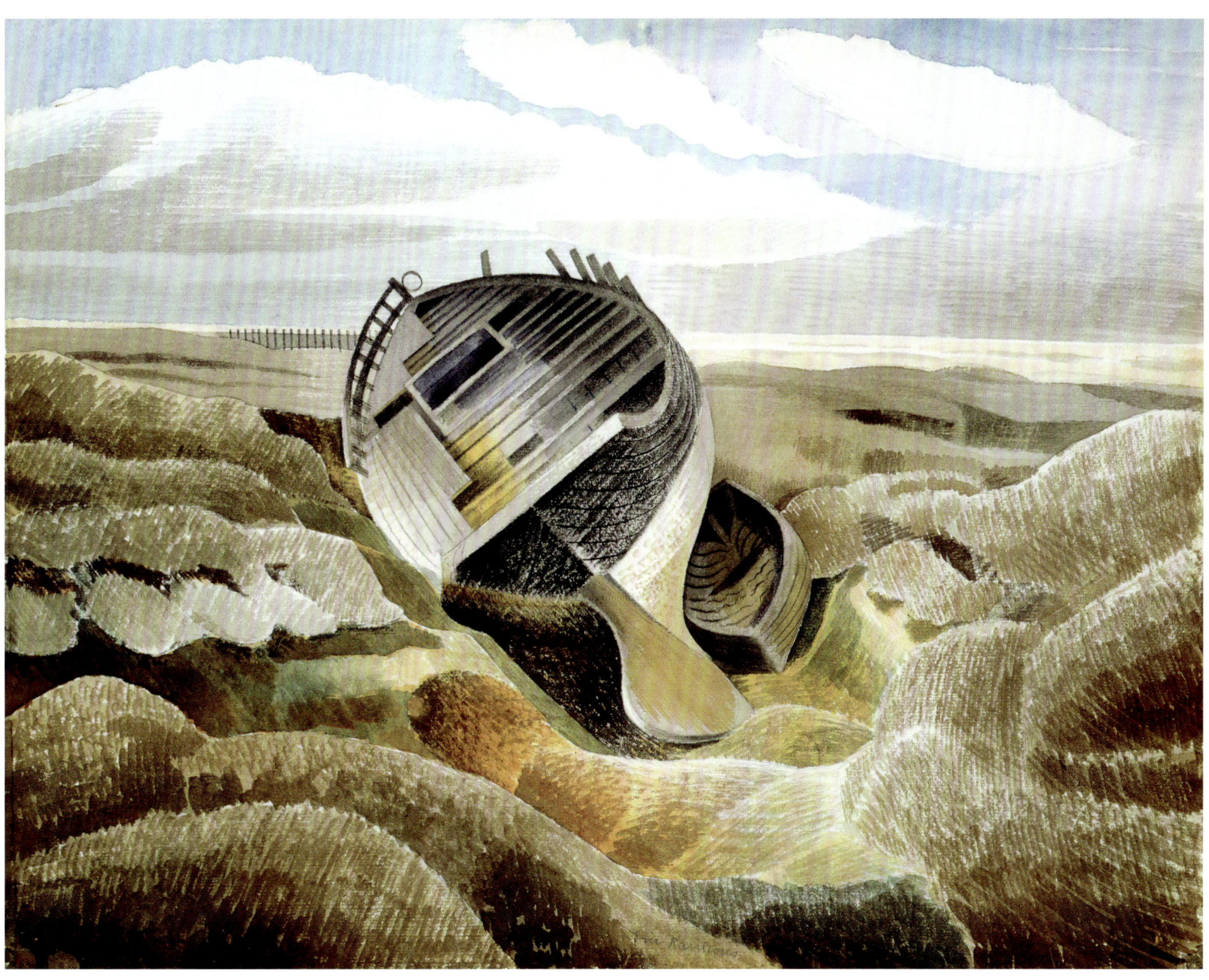

LATE AUGUST BEACH

Ravilious once wrote to Helen Binyon of 'the restlessness that is one of my besetting sins', and the 18 months leading up to his 1939 exhibition of watercolours saw him travel from Wales to northern France in search of inspiration. True to his liking for series, he painted a number of coastal scenes, including two paintings of Aldeburgh's flamboyant, blue-and-white-striped bathing machines, which had been photographed back in 1860 and were evidently still in good repair shortly before World War II.

The first bathing machines appeared in the mid-18th century, when the Hanoverian kings began to make sea bathing fashionable. A swimmer climbed aboard the machine while it was parked on the beach, changed into a bathing suit and then sat tight as the machine was pulled, pushed or, more unusually, winched down to the sea. Until the Edwardian period these remarkable devices could be found at every seaside resort, but with the abolition of segregated swimming in 1901 they soon became obsolete, making those painted by Ravilious an extreme rarity. One does still survive today at Aldeburgh, though without its wheels.

With paintings like this on display, the artist's third solo show enjoyed a rapturous reception by critics and art collectors, and this success in turn allowed him to return to the coast in 1940 to sketch, in his role of War Artist, the barbed wire, concrete pillboxes and submerged girders of coastal defence.

Before the outbreak of war, however, there was still one summer to enjoy, and time for Ravilious to indulge in a favourite seasonal pastime. Readers of *Wisden Cricketers' Almanack* may recall the cover illustration of Victorian gentlemen playing cricket; still in use today, this image is based on a wood engraving made by Ravilious in 1938. He enjoyed watching cricket and in 1935 played for the Double Crown Club against the village at the ground on St James's St, Castle Hedingham. The following day Ravilious reported that he was 'not out, hit four balls, and made 1, also bowled a few overs and in consequence feel stiff as a poker...

'It all felt just like being back at school,' he added, 'especially the trestle tea with slabs of bread and butter and that wicked looking cheap cake.'

A few weeks before the outbreak of war a less formal game brought together friends from Castle Hedingham and beyond, including Robert and Kay Goodden, Guy and Evelyn Hepher, Jim Richards and Ravilious himself. This time Ravilious was delighted to hit three sixes, it being 'one of the pleasures of life hitting a six.

'The team made 160 altogether,' he wrote, 'and finished just as a storm broke, and we all had to make a race downhill for claret cup at the Bell... It was a well made claret cup and plenty of it.'

Late August Beach, 1938, watercolour, 39 x 52 cm, private collection.

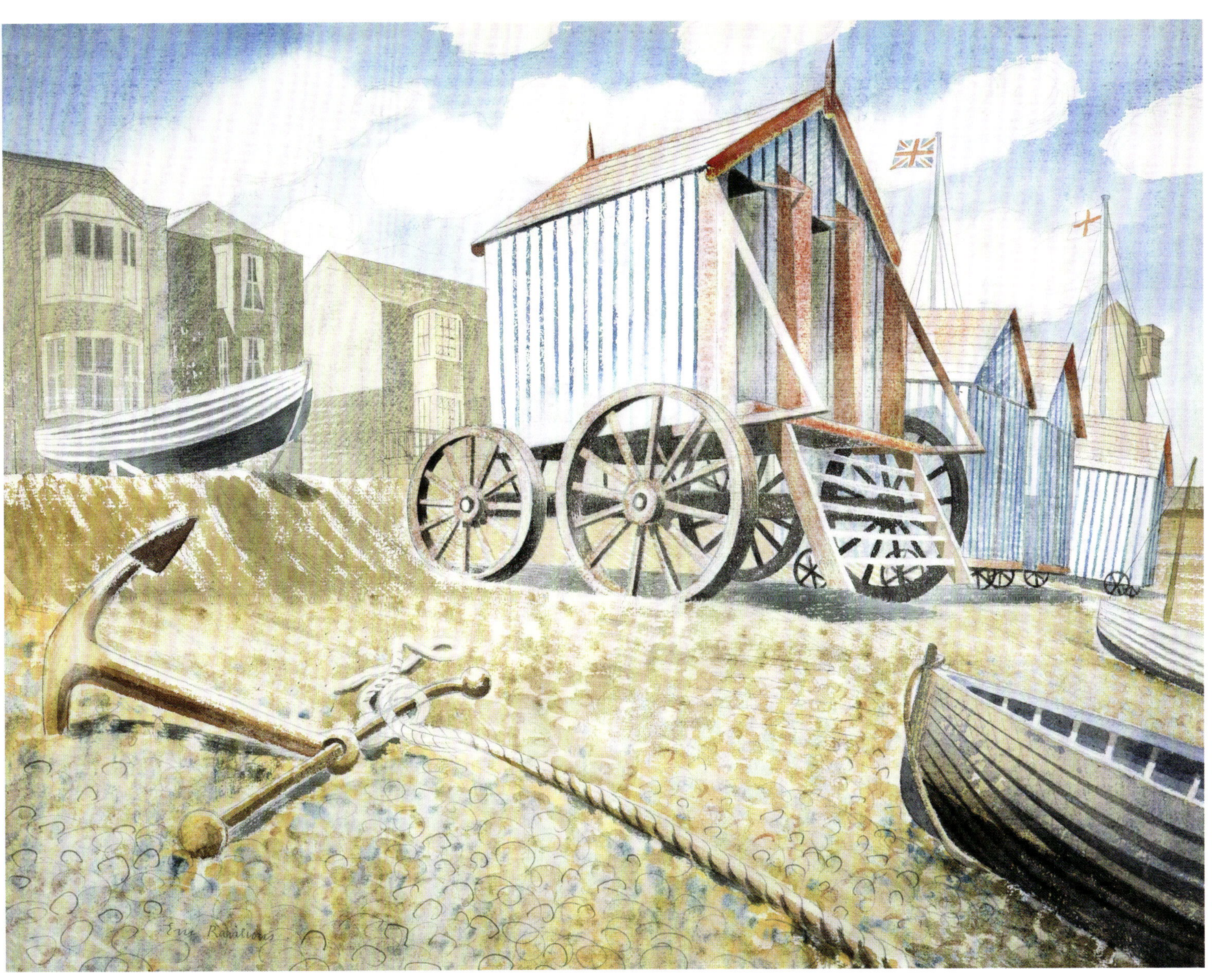

IRONBRIDGE INTERIOR

With the outbreak of war in September 1939, life in north-west Essex changed as it did everywhere. Bawden and Ravilious were appointed as War Artists, while Kay Goodden became a Land Girl before joining the WAAF. Evacuees, soldiers and wounded men came and went. The first winter of the war saw the severest frosts since 1894, causing Ravilious to remark, 'I've now seen ink, milk, and soda water frozen.'

The following winter was as bad, and at Bank House pipes froze – forcing the family to seek refuge at the vicarage – then burst, flooding the ground floor. On 1 April 1941 Tirzah gave birth to their third child, Anne, and soon afterwards the family left plumbing disasters behind (or so they thought) and moved to Ironbridge Farm, outside Shalford and not far from Great Bardfield. The move was apparently engineered by Ariel Crittall, who was a friend both of the Ravilious family and of John Strachey, the eminent left-wing author and politician, and his wife Celia.

A timber-framed, 16th-century building, Ironbridge Farm was beautiful but dilapidated. The Stracheys bought the place in the mid-1930s as an investment, intending to renovate and then resell it, and using the house as a country retreat in the meantime. When a German invasion seemed imminent, however, Celia and their children Charles and Lou were evacuated to Canada, for fear that their father's outspoken opposition to Fascism would endanger them. The house was left empty.

Ariel Crittall had been appalled when, on a visit to Bank House, she saw three frogs jump out of a cupboard under the stairs, and she suggested the family leave the damp house and rent Ironbridge instead. The military had their eye on the place too, but Ravilious beat them to it and worked out with Strachey an arrangement whereby he paid half the rent in cash and half in paintings. The new tenant set to work right away, painting this interior.

A deep tranquillity emanates from this room with its bare walls and plain furniture. Soft light seeps in at the window, while beyond the glass a pale mist conceals the outside world, leaving only the faint outline of trees. A partially-finished painting is pinned to one wall, showing a second still life and reinforcing the impression that this room is a refuge from the upheaval and suffering caused by the war, a timeless space in which the mind and the eye can contemplate the jug with its intriguing, snake-like decoration and the simple arrangement of country flowers.

'There is a great quiet in the house,' Tirzah wrote not long after, when her mother was staying, 'broken only by cries and quacks of different birds. You'll like these birds, they come into the passage much to mummy's indignation. I can hear them there now.'

Ironbridge Interior, 1941, watercolour, 46.9 x 55.9 cm, private collection, on loan to the Towner Art Gallery, Eastbourne.

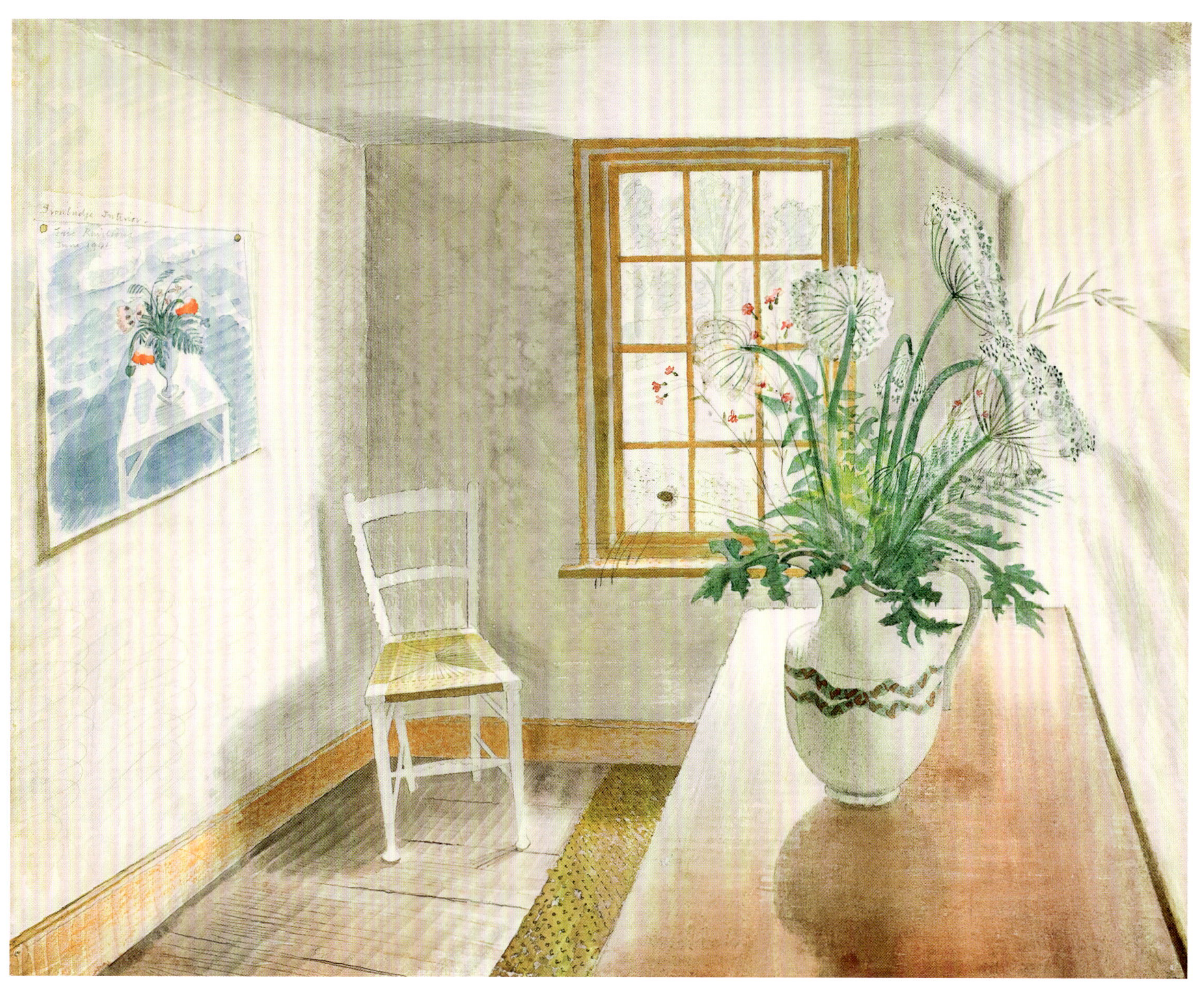

TREE TRUNK AND WHEELBARROW

The sawn trunk of a tree lies in a field littered with twigs and sticks, beside a wheelbarrow filled with foliage. Beyond it a building stands with timbers exposed and tarpaulins for a roof, while a greenhouse and walled garden can be seen to the right. The bareness of the land suggests that this is winter – a fact confirmed by a letter written to Helen Binyon in February, in which Ravilious explains that the pipes are frozen and the family away.

'So I've been by myself painting landscapes and jolly cold work it has been too, and I come in and make huge log fires and drink tea. It is fun trying to paint landscape again and these fallen trees are splendid things with beautiful pale yellow sections. Naples yellow is the colour with a rind of sienna.'

Not for the first time Ravilious presents us with a scene from which the human inhabitants seem to have mysteriously vanished. It is hard to say which is the more disturbing, the building with its exposed timbers or the tree trunk itself, but the signs are ominous.

'I'm afraid we've had an unfortunate winter at Ironbridge,' Tirzah wrote in March, in a letter to John Strachey.

'John and the baby nearly died of whooping cough when we all had it in the autumn… Now James has just had measles and I have had a major operation, turned a startling blue and had to have a blood transfusion.' Tirzah had been rushed into hospital for an emergency mastectomy only two weeks before she wrote this letter, after being diagnosed with cancer. Now she gave full vent to her pain and her frustration at the farm's terrible plumbing, the frozen pipes, leaking sink and 'constant water under the sitting room floor'. Ought they, she wondered, to contact 'old Mr Bawden of Crittall and Winterton' for help? It was 'his first bit of plumbing that he did as a boy so he feels a certain amount of sentimental attachment for it we may hope'.

This was Edward's father – employee, manager and eventually owner of the respected Braintree ironmongers – but whether he ever came to look at the plumbing we do not know. Tirzah's letter was never sent, and with the spring, life at Ironbridge Farm improved once again.

'You would like this place,' Ravilious wrote in April to Alathea Fry. 'It is 50 yards from the river and the nicest sort of Essex farmhouse, with white weatherboarding on the south side: only it is too remote for winter living. I think we shall have to move though I don't much like the idea of moving, but it is too hard a life for Tirzah here with these Victorian winters. I wish you could see Ironbridge. It is one of the nicest houses I've lived in, perfect for the children.'

Tree Trunk and Wheelbarrow, 1942, watercolour, 49.5 x 54.6 cm, private collection.

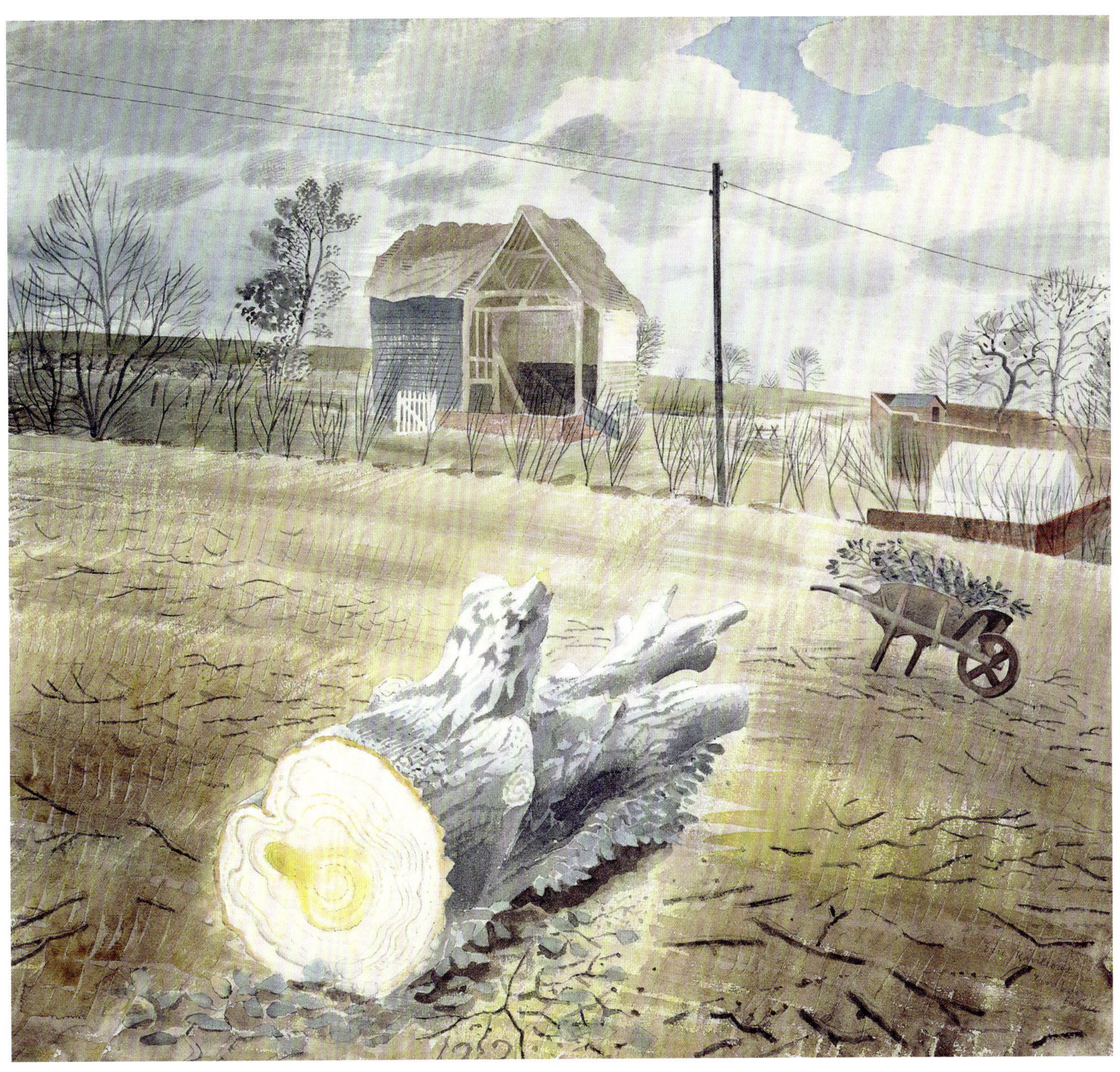

Beneath bare winter branches a bridge leads across a stream to open country beyond. For a rural footbridge this is an impressive structure, with iron railings and posts supported by elegant iron hoops, but on closer inspection it appears that the bridge was built not for human traffic but for sheep. The ground in front of the bridge is well worn, the hill beyond ideal for grazing. The name too is suggestive. Charles Strachey recalls that his family always referred to the farm as Ewenbridge and, despite a lack of hard evidence, believes that the site may mark an ancestral crossing place for livestock.

This was one of several watercolours Ravilious painted in lieu of rent; it is unlikely that we would have any pictures of Ironbridge – or, for that matter, any non-war-related paintings from this period – if the arrangement had not been in place. And this is an exquisite piece, one that celebrates good, everyday design and workmanship while inviting an imaginative response. A fairytale troll might live beneath this bridge; a pilgrim might cross to the other side. The elegant ironwork suggests a faith in the power of good design to carry us safely into the future.

In September 1942, only months after completing this painting, Ravilious was reported missing off the coast of Iceland. Still weak from surgery, Tirzah now found the government reluctant to pay either her late husband's outstanding salary or her widow's pension. She was forced to argue her case repeatedly, until she finally received the money owed to her a year later and was able to concentrate on the business of living. She began painting in oils, and in 1946 married BBC man Henry Swanzy. However, her cancer returned and she died in March 1951, with Anne not quite 10 years old.

Here the story takes a twist in keeping with Ravilious's optimistic nature. With the upheavals of the war, their old Hedingham friend Kay Goodden had parted from her first husband Robert, and by coincidence married Henry Swanzy's brother John. On Tirzah's death Kay and John took the Ravilious children in, and gave them a stable and happy home.

This future lay ahead, unseen, as Ravilious sketched the bridge. He was at Ironbridge on and off during the summer, as the farm became idyllic once again. In June he reported, 'The river here looks lovely and I bathed today. The old man Brown who keeps the boats wears a battered old Panama and stinging vermilion football jersey in these grey-green willows.'

He came and went, returning for the last time in August to find the children waiting. 'The Baffy (James) and Anne were at Overall's corner when I returned...' he wrote, 'James chasing a cat and Anne laughing with joy to see her father.'

Ironbridge at Ewenbridge, 1942, watercolour, 55.2 x 50.1 cm, private collection, on loan to the Towner Art Gallery, Eastbourne.

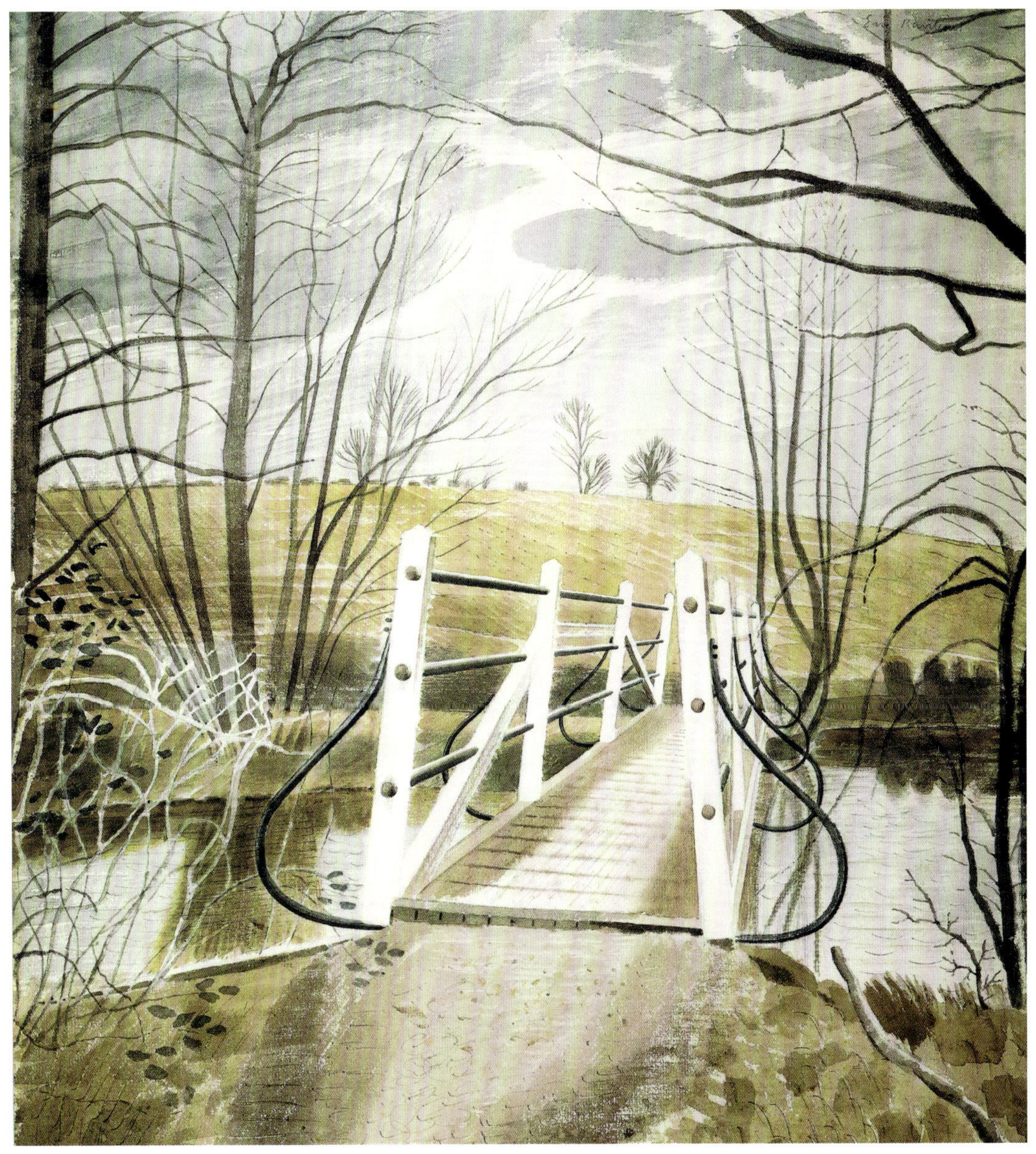

First published in April 2011 by
The Mainstone Press, Vivian Road, London E3 5RF
www.themainstonepress.com

ISBN 978-0955277764

Edited by Tim Mainstone / Design by Webb & Webb
Printed by Graphicom, Italy

The wood engravings by Eric Ravilious used throughout *A Country Life*
were cut for the Kynoch Press Notebook, 1933

We are indebted to Anne Ullmann, the artist's daughter, and to Simon
Lawrence of The Fleece Press. Quotations from the correspondence of
Eric Ravilious are mostly taken from their book *Eric Ravilious: Landscape,
Letters and Design* published by The Fleece Press in 2008. We would like to
thank Adrian Corder-Birch for his invaluable help in researching this book.
Thanks also to Robin Ravilious, Brian Webb, Sara Cooper, Matthew Rowe,
Susanna and Alan Powers, Joe Pearson, Carol and John Mainstone, Nigel
and Iris Weaver, Liz Barrett, David Collidge, Charles Strachey and Gordon
Cummings for their assistance and support.

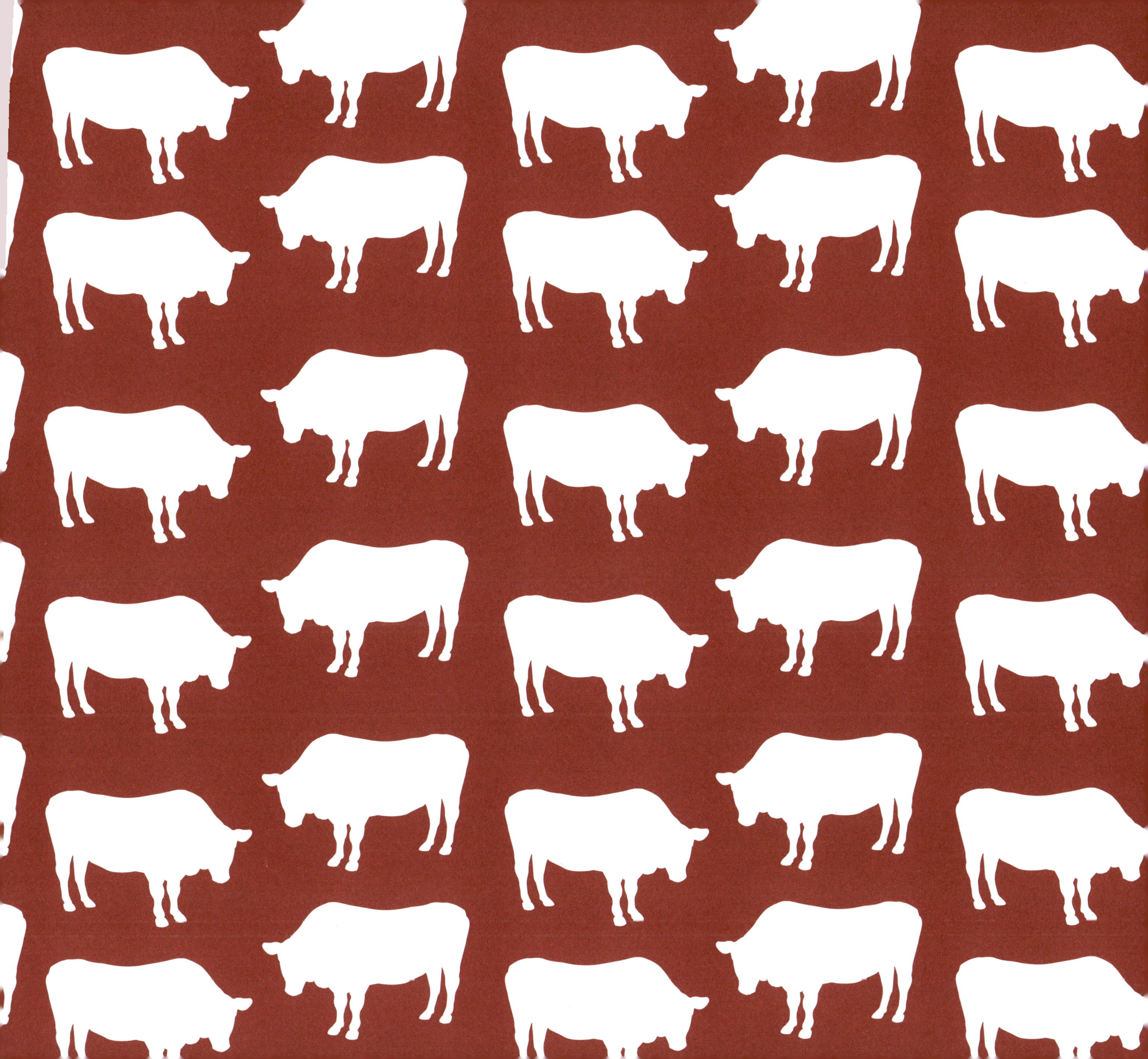

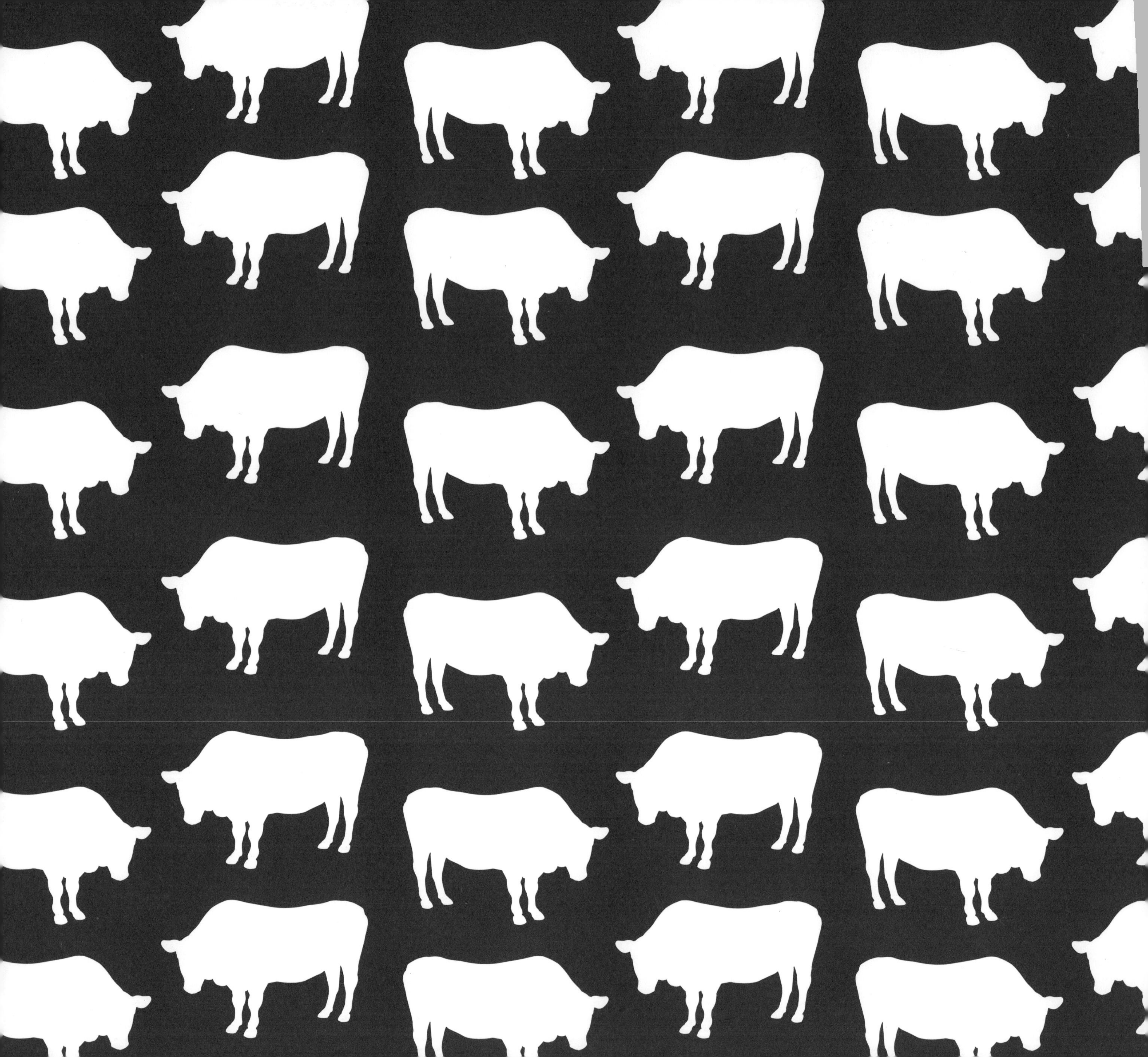